The Life
That Wins

The Life That Wins

WATCHMAN NEE

Christian Fellowship Publishers, Inc.
New York

Available from the Publishers at:

11515 Allecingie Parkway
Richmond, Virginia 23235

Printed in the United States of America

TRANSLATOR'S PREFACE

Do you know the life that wins? Are you ashamed of the kind of Christian life you live? Have you failed so terribly in your striving for victory that you cry out, "Wretched man that I am! who shall deliver me . . . ?" (Rom. 7.24) Be assured that your salvation is at hand: "thank God through Jesus Christ our Lord" (v.25). For the life that wins is not attained, but obtained. It is not a life changed, but rather a life exchanged. It is not suppression, only expression. It is frankly not in you yourself, because it is in Christ who lives in you. The life which God gives and you receive at the time you believe in His Son Jesus Christ is such a life. It is a life that overcomes sin, provides intimate communion with God, and is full of satisfaction and power. It is already in you, waiting to be explored by you. The secret towards experiencing its power is to let go of yourself and let Christ live instead of you. This requires a childlike faith. Then shall you more than conquer through Him who loves you.

In order to help believers into enjoying this life that wins, Watchman Nee delivered a series of messages on this subject at a conference held in Shanghai, China, in the months of September and October, 1935. He dealt with the full range of this important subject in his usual thoroughness yet simplicity and directness. At that conference, the author began with the believer's personal experience which, shamefully, is much less than desired. Then, by contrast, he described the kind of Christian life as ordained by God. Next, he dealt with the nature of this life that wins before he showed the way of entering into it. In more detail, he treated the matters of yielding and believing, which are the conditions for crossing the threshold of victory. But the author of these messages then warned his audience of the testing of faith which must follow. He exhorted believers to grow in the grace of Jesus Christ. He stressed also the need for having the note of triumph, which is praise. And finally, he concluded with the first and last act after victory, which is consecration.

These messages are now being translated from the Chinese for the first time and presented to the readers in book form. May the Lord of glory be glorified through His life being lived out in His own.

CONTENTS

1 | Our Experience

I find then the law, that, to me who would do good, evil is present. (Rom. 7.21)

All have sinned, and fall short of the glory of God. (Rom. 3.23)

The Life Ordained for Christians

From the Holy Scriptures we may see that the life as ordained by God for Christians is one full of joy and rest, one that is uninterrupted communion with God, and is in perfect harmony with His will. It is a life that does not thirst and hunger after the world, that walks outside of sins, and that transcends all things. Indeed, it is a holy, powerful and victorious life, and one that constitutes knowing God's will and having continuous fellowship with Him.

The life which God has ordained for Christians is a life that is hid with Christ in God. Nothing can touch, affect or shake this life. As Christ is unshakable, so we are unshakable. As Christ transcends all things, we also transcend all things. As Christ is before God, so we too are before Him. Let us never entertain the thought that we should be weak and defeated. There is no such thing as weakness and defeat; for "Christ is our life" as declared in Colossians 3.4. He transcends all; He cannot be touched by anything. Hallelujah! This is the life of Christ!

The life ordained for Christians is full of rest, full of joy, full of power, and full of the will of God. But let us inquire of ourselves as to what sort of life we are living today. If our life is not what God has ordained it to be, then we need to know victory. Hence, we shall look into this matter of our experience. And what we shall relate here may not be pleasing to our ears, because some of us are rather pathetic; yet we need to humble ourselves in order that we may see our lack and receive grace from God.

Eight Kinds of Failures among Christians

What kind of life are we living? Do we live under the bondage of the law of sin? Is it true in our experience that "to will is present with me, but to do that which is good is not" (Rom. 7.18)? Is our life defeated and bound by sin? God gives us such a glorious life, and yet we live in defeat. According to the record of the Scriptures and as concurred in by our experience, we may conclude from our investigation that there are eight different kinds of failure or sin to be seen in Christians.

1. Sins of the Spirit. Pride, jealousy, unbelief, fault-finding, lack of prayer, and an inability to commit oneself to God—all these are sins of the spirit. Though some Christians are spiritually victorious, others find themselves defeated in this particular area.

Pride itself had once troubled me. All who are proud have committed this sin of the spirit. A proud person is unable to consider others as more excellent than he. This is not only true in worldly matters but is also true in spiritual ones. If anyone else seems to be superior to the proud person in spiritual things, the latter will always try to find fault with that one. He will attempt to put him down.

Jealousy is sin, whether it appears in work or in spiritual matters.

Some are filled with an evil heart of unbelief. If a person is asked if he believes, he will answer that he believes in every word of God. But if he be questioned as to whether he really believes in God's promise, he finds himself unable to believe. A little trial will upset him, because he cannot trust God's word. On one occasion Martin Luther's wife had put on mourning dress and then challenged her husband with these words: "I have put on mourning dress today because you worry so much as though to say that your God is dead." Is the same true of us in our day?

. Many do not live before God and maintain good communion with Him. They live carelessly day after day. They may spend days on end without prayer and Bible reading. They can exist a whole week without ever seeing God's face in fellowship with Him. Day after day they live without any fear of the Lord. This shows that they lack living before God. They have no spiritual life. They have never learned the lesson of dealing with self. They have never denied themselves.

Once, two brothers quarreled over a rather small matter. As they would eat together, one brother would always pick out a few of the best-looking pieces of meat first. The other brother noticed this act. He kept silence for a day or two, but after two weeks this other brother could bear it no more and separated himself from his brother. Let me observe that the kind of person one is is often revealed not in the large but in the small things. In this regard, I am reminded of the biography of Hudson Taylor, which I love to read. As he would travel here and there to preach the gospel, the worst room and the worst bed would always seemingly turn out to be his. Yet this missionary servant of God never murmured or complained. Though this was but a small issue, nonetheless, one's reaction to such small matters reveals what kind of life one lives before God.

2. Sins of the Flesh. There are not only sins of the spirit, there are also sins of the flesh—such as adultery, unrestrained eyes, and unnatural relationships. Many fail in these matters. How many sin with their eyes, for they never control their looking. Many maintain improper friendships. Some sins of the flesh pertain to the body, whereas other sins do not.

Have you ever controlled your eyes? I acknowledge that there is much opportunity to see with the eyes in these days. We must deal with this matter before God. I know many Christians who cannot enter into victory because they fail to deal with their eyes.

Friendship is also a matter to be reckoned with here. A certain brother maintained a friendship with an unbeliever above all others. Such conduct is not viewed as a sin in the eyes of the world, but to us who are Christians it *is* a sin. A missionary once testified that he refused someone's friendship because the latter asked for a friendship above all others.

3. Sins of the Mind. Many may not commit sins of the spirit, and they also may have their flesh dealt with; yet they have no victory in their mind. Their thoughts drift, wander, and are scattered. Some find their thoughts to be unclean or too imaginative or full of doubt or full of curiosity. They want to know everything; they cannot abide the unknown. Those who have this kind of mind have not entered into victorious living. As a matter of fact, few actually experience victory in their mind at all. Once I met a sister who wondered why her thoughts always drifted. I also met a brother who confessed that his thoughts were continually unclean. We must deal with this area if we want to live out the life of God.

Imagination or doubt damages many Christians. Suppose, for example, you meet a brother on the street whose face appears to be somewhat unpleasant; immediately you surmise that he must be unhappy with you. But upon reaching his home, you come to learn that he has not slept well and his head is aching. You had imagined he had something against you, but actually it was not that at all.

How we are hurt by imagination, yet we consider ourselves to be most discerning. Let us remember that only our Lord "searcheth the reins and hearts" (Rev. 2.23). Many falsely imagine so and so is such and such. By so doing, we have sinned in our mind. We pronounce too much judgment and imagine too much for our own good. We must deal with our minds before God, else how can we possibly enter into the life that wins?

One brother was filled with an inordinate desire to know. And because he had to know the reason for everything, he analyzed everything. His mind was truly overactive; but because he knew everything, he could not trust God. Such desire for knowledge, like these other areas of the mind, truly needs to be dealt with.

4. Sins of the Body. Certain activities centering upon the physical body may be overlooked by the world, but to spiritually sensitive Christians they may nonetheless be sinful. Some pay too much attention to eating or sleeping or hygiene or adornment or life itself. These can be sinful in God's sight.

Many Christians just *have* to eat; they have never fasted once since becoming Christians. Eating with them will tell you immediately what kind of person they are. As they lift up the knife and fork, you know at once what they really are. One brother I have met, for example, said that his appetite was big and special. Yet I must say here that a lack of self-control in the matter of eating can also be a sin.

Some sleep just a little less than usual and they automatically look unhappy. And consequently, they become hasty in works and muddled in speech. This too is sin.

Some love to munch on food; so they spend lots of money on snacks. Others like to adorn themselves at all times. And there are some who are so hygienically minded that they are continually obsessed with a sense of danger. What is all this? It is loving of one's own life. Many love their own life so much that they cannot bear the slightest suffering or to come too near the sick. To put it quite frankly, they are under bondage to their body. Yet Paul said this: "I buffet my body, and lead it captive!" (see 1 Cor.

9.27) If we allow our body to dominate us, that is sin. Our body should be *under* us, not above us. Many sacrifice morning prayer because they want to sleep. Many sacrifice the time for reading the Bible because they want to eat. Many cannot serve God because they covet snacks and indulge in adornment. Lack of control over these areas of the body is sinful.

5. Sins of Disposition. Disposition makes an individual. Everyone is born with a particular kind. This constitutes his special character. Nevertheless, the Lord comes to save us from our disposition as well as from our sins. Some people are born with hard and brittle characters, while others are born with a most righteous attitude. The latter kind of person acts as though he were the judge of the supreme court in all matters for all people at all times. He may indeed be most righteous in his constitution, but he lacks gentleness and sweetness in his dealings with brethren. He is very righteous but he is too hard. Let me say that this also is sin.

Just the opposite to the righteous man who is hard is the person who is very weak and most fearful of anything. So that to him everything is all right. People may deem such a "goodie-goodie" person as this to be holy, but we need to ask how many such persons have been used by God? Was the Son of God a "goodie-goodie" while on earth? The answer obviously is no. Such sins in disposition as represented by these two kinds of people need to be dealt with.

Then again, though, some brother may be neither hard nor soft but desires to be head. Wherever he is, he must display himself. No matter what the circumstance, he always has to speak or to be the center of attention. He will not be satisfied until he is noticed by people. He wants to project himself constantly; he cannot be a hidden person.

Still another believer is most timid and withdrawn. Wherever this person is, he or she always sits in the corner and refuses to come forth. This too is a sinful disposition and needs to be dealt with.

Some Christians are quick-tempered. One brother once said, "I thank God that though I lose my temper quickly, I also stop quickly. In the morning I may lose my temper, but after five minutes it is all over. I forget it all when I arrive at my office." Yet in the wake of his hot temper, his wife and children must suffer the entire day. And when he returns home he wonders why his wife is miserable, whereas he himself has felt quite good. This conduct is sinful and must be dealt with.

Now while some people are quick-tempered, others are never hasty. They can let a thing go undone for a day or even ten days. This is a form of laziness and should be dealt with.

Everybody has his own particular disposition or temperament. Though a person may be saved, he may be very sharp in his reaction. He is strict and tight in relation to every matter. Though he would never defraud others, he will make very sure that others will not be allowed to defraud him. He would never hurt a person's eye or tooth, but should anyone ever try to hurt *his* eye or tooth, then it will become for him a matter of eye for eye and tooth for tooth!

Others may not be as sharp as this man, but they may turn out to be very mean. They may not actually rob people; nonetheless, if an opportunity presents itself for them to take advantage of others, they will do so, even if it would only be a matter of a few pennies involved.

By nature some persons may be very talkative. When such people are present there can be no silence, and what is worse they always talk about other people. If they know anything, they must speak out. Though they have no intention of telling a lie, they will nonetheless often exaggerate. Such is their disposition in speech. Let us all understand that if we desire to be overcomers, we must allow the Lord to deal with us on these matters of personal character.

Why do I speak about these things? It is because the life lived by many Christians is too unlike the life of God. Some brethren can only see people's faults; they cannot see any of the good qualities in others. They always talk about the shortcomings of their fellow-brethren. For instance, a brother who had finally gained victory over this matter confessed beforehand that he did not understand why he always found fault with his brethren. He would look at a brother and find six or seven faults in him; he would look at another brother, and again, he would find in that brother six or seven faults. I told him that the reason why he did this was because he himself had these same faults: that this was how his own disposition was.

All these faults in disposition, character and temperament are sins, and every Christian must live victoriously above these things, not be defeated under them.

6. No Heart to Keep God's Word. From the viewpoint of the Scriptures what some of us lack before God is not having a heart to keep His word. This too is a sin. Let us ask ourselves how many of God's commands we have read and obeyed. For instance, how many husbands love their wives, and how many wives are subject to their husbands? One wife confessed that she knew she should submit to her husband, but in every instance she submitted only after she had first quarreled with him. She today realizes that she had never really submitted according to God's command.

How many Christians know that worry is sin? "Rejoice in the Lord always," declares the Scripture (Phil. 4.4). How many Christians have kept this commandment? We should acknowledge that worry or anxiety is sin. All who refuse to rejoice have committed sin, for the commandment of God is that "in nothing" are we to "be anxious" (Phil. 4.6). If you worry, you sin. Though worry is not considered sinful in man's eyes, it is a sin according to the word of God.

We ought to give thanks in all things, for such is God's commandment. In all things we should pray: "O God, I thank You, and I praise You." Even if we have met with difficulty, we still should say: "O God, I praise You." There was a story about a woman with nine children. She argued that surely the word "in nothing be anxious" could not possibly be applied to a mother like her, since to her, *not* to worry was sin. She had first had two children for whom she had continually worried until they died; and she then had had seven more to worry about concerning their progress towards maturity. Alas, this woman failed to see that worry was indeed a sin, whereas she had falsely imagined worry to be her Christian duty.

It is God's commandment that we "rejoice always" (1 Thess. 5.16). It is also His will that we do not worry about anything. It is equally His will that "in everything" we are to "give thanks" (1 Thess. 5.18a). All who overcome have the strength to keep God's commandment. Only those who do not overcome cannot keep His will.

7. Failure to Render to God His Due. God demands that we present ourselves—together with our families, businesses and wealth—wholly to Him. It seems, however, that every Christian tries to retain something for himself. Let us understand that although under the Old Covenant the people had to offer *one*-tenth to God, the New Covenant offering is *ten*-tenths. We ought to offer our houses, fields, wives, children, and our very selves altogether to the Lord.

Many Christians are fearful lest God trouble them. Once a believer who was afraid of offering himself to the Lord said, "If I offer myself to God, and He makes me suffer, what can I do?" To which I replied quite seriously: "Who do you think God is? Suppose a child who used to disobey his parents said to them that hereafter he will obey them. Do you think his parents will deliberately require him to do what he cannot do so as to make him suffer? If so, they are not parents, but judges. Being parents, they doubtless will be especially merciful to their child. How, then, can you suggest that God would purposely cause you to suffer? Do you really think He would intentionally destroy you? You forget that He is your *Father.*"

Let me make clear to you that the consecrated one alone has power. He places his business in God's hand; he puts his parents, wife and children in His hand also. His wealth too is in God's hand. The consecrated one could never take what the Lord has given him and deposit it in the world. On the contrary, he offers himself and all that he has to God. Whoever is afraid to lay all (including people, things and affairs) before God in consecration cannot be an overcomer. The more a person offers to the Lord, the greater will be that person's power. For the one who willingly offers to the Lord seems to press things into His hand, asking Him to take more in. Consecration makes life powerful as well as joyful. He who is unwilling to offer to God is powerless, joyless, and sinful.

8. Unrepentant of Sins That Require Confession. Some may have dealt with many other matters, but they refuse to confess with their heart that there are sins in their lives. This is what is meant by the phrase in Psalm 66.18 to "regard iniquity in [the] heart." The heart not only longs for but even loves the sin, and is thus unable to get rid of it. There is that secret love in the heart for this or that sin, and an unwillingness to confess it. Though one may not speak out loud that he loves the sin and may not even move towards it with his feet, his heart is nonetheless already there. Oftentimes sin is not a matter of outward conduct but of inward desire. Whoever regards iniquity in his heart needs victory.

Many not only love sin in their hearts, they also have sins which remain unconfessed. How often you sin against a brother, and whenever you think about it you acknowledge to yourself that you have offended him. So that henceforth you try to change your *outward attitude* towards him by being especially kind to him: you shake his hand when you meet, and you receive him with diligence. Let me say that changing your attitude is *your* best way,

but it is not at all *God's* way. His way is not a change in your
outward attitude. What God expects is for you to confess your sin.

Now with regard to confessing sin, the Bible does not teach
that we must confess in detail. It only instructs us to *confess* the
sin, not to tell the *detailed* story of it to others. "If thy brother
sin against thee" (Matt. 18.15a). He may sin against you in a
number of things. But when he comes to confess, he only needs
to say, "Brother, I have sinned against you," and you must forgive
him. There is no need for the one who comes to you to tell the
hidden stories, because no human ear is worthy to hear all these
stories.

Let me ask you, how many sins do you still regard in your
heart? How many iniquities are yet there? If there *are* such sins,
you need victory, else you will not be able to live a life that wins.

Victory Is Necessary As Well As Possible

If you have these eight kinds of sin as just outlined above,
you need victory for sure. I do not know how many of these eight
kinds of sin you may have. Perhaps only one or two of them continues to entangle you, perhaps more. Nevertheless, God will
consent to allow neither many or one of these sins to entangle
you. Such a situation ought not to exist; it is clearly unnecessary.
I thank and praise God, because whatever sin it may be, it is
under your feet. Thank the Lord that no sin is so strong that you
have to yield to it. Thank Him that no temptation is too great to
overcome.

The life which the Lord has ordained for us is one of un-
shadowed communion with Him, of doing the will of God, and
of total detachment from all contrary things. Every Christian
is absolutely able to overcome sins of the mind, body, flesh and
spirit, our contrary disposition, unbelief, and even the love of
sin. Thank and praise God, this is not an unobtainable, ideal
life under consideration here. This is a totally practical way of
living which all of us may have in experience.

Honest in Heart, Not Deceiving Oneself

We must ask God to deliver us from deceiving ourselves. For He can only bless one class of people — those who possess an honest heart before Him. It is said that God will bless those who do not lie to Him. If you honestly say to Him, "O God, I did lie before, but I ask Your forgiveness," He will immediately bless you.

Perhaps you as an unsatisfied Christian are asking God to satisfy you. Let me frankly tell you that the one who is unsatisfied may not necessarily be the *hungry* one. In order to be satisfied, we must first be hungry. The prodigal left his father's home, wasted all he had, and later longed to fill his belly with the husks which the swine were eating; but no one gave to him. This is a being unsatisfied. Some, though, may be filled with husks, yet they remain unsatisfied every day. Hence being unsatisfied is one thing, whereas being hungry is another. How can we be satisfied if we are often weak and frequently defeated? We may be unsatisfied, yes; but we still live such a life from dawn to dusk. Consequently, it is better that we be hungry instead of being merely unsatisfied. For God can only bless those who are hungry. He has no obligation to fulfill the merely unsatisfied.

Let us today stop lying, for we have lied long enough before God. Let us acknowledge that we have failed before Him. Our confession before men will glorify God's name. Praise and thank the Lord, all who are honest will receive blessing. May many be met by God and be blessed.

2 | The Christian Life As Revealed in Scripture

Blessed be the God and Father of our Lord Jesus Christ, who hath blessed us with every spiritual blessing in the heavenly places in Christ. (Eph. 1.3)

The Christian's Experience of Defeat

When we were first saved our hearts were filled with joy because of the grace of God. We had great hope for our life. We thought that henceforth we could tread all sins under our feet. We reckoned that from now on we would walk a victorious path. No temptation could be too great for us to overcome. No problem could be too difficult for us to solve. Our future was full of glorious hope, because at that time we tasted the peace and joy of sins forgiven for the very first time. Our communion with God was effortless and sweet. We were truly full of joy; we felt heaven was very close to us. It seemed that nothing was impossible to us. We fully believed that day after day we would live victoriously.

Unfortunately, such a beautiful condition does not last long; and this glorious expectation is not fulfilled. The sins which you dreamed were already overcome find their way back again. Sins which once could not touch you have now returned. Your old temper, pride and jealousy raise their ugly heads once more. You read God's word much, but you get no help. You pray, yet you lose the intimate taste you once enjoyed. Your zeal for the lost also decreases, and your love grows cold. You may be able to deal with some matters, but you find that certain others are beyond your strength. Your daily note is now defeat, not victory. In fact, in your daily life you experience more defeats than victories. You sense your great lack. As you compare yourself with Paul, John, Peter and those other Christians in the first century, you know how different they were from you. You are unable to help other people. You may tell them the stories of your *victories*, but you dare not tell them the stories of your *defeats*. You feel your days of victory are short while your days of defeat are long. And consequently, you pass your time in sorrow. Such is the experience which many Christians share.

When we are saved, we surmise that since our sins are forgiven they will never find us again. We honestly believe that the joy and peace we now enjoy will remain with us forever. Who would therefore imagine that sin as well as temptation might ever return? Who would ever expect that there might later be more lows than highs? Who would ever dream there might be more sorrows than joys awaiting us sometime down the road? Yet, when temptation, pride, jealousy, ill temper or whatever do come back we will usually do two things: we will either exert our utmost strength to suppress sin, or else we will take the attitude that it is impossible to overcome. As these sins return, we on the one hand may exert much effort to suppress them so that they will not appear outwardly: whoever among us is able to control or suppress them will consider himself to be victorious. But on the other hand, those of us who are defeated spend our days in defeat and victory, victory and defeat, sinning and repenting, repenting and sinning: it is a life of continuously making a circle which only ends in our falling into deep despair. Hence, if we succeed in controlling sin, we merely suppress it for a time; or if we fail to suppress it, we consider sinning to be unavoidable and plunge into despair and a wringing of our hands.

Yet I need to ask you in the presence of the God whom I serve: When our Lord Jesus went to the cross on our behalf, did

He have in view for our future the kind of experience we too often go through today? As He was being crucified, did He envision our current living as that which would be success in the morning but failure in the afternoon? Is the work He has fully accomplished on the cross not enough to enable us to serve Him in holiness and righteousness? Did the Lord shed His blood on the cross because He only saw the penalty of hell without seeing as well the pain of sinning? Does the blood He shed on the cross only save us from the sufferings of the future but leave the sufferings of today for us to bear?

Oh! At this point I cannot help but shout, Hallelujah! for our Lord has accomplished *all* at Calvary! While He was on the cross, He thought not only of the penalty of hell but also of the pain of sin. He foresaw the sufferings due to the power of sin as well as those due to its penalty. He has a salvation which enables us to live on earth as He once lived on earth. In other words, Christ's work of redemption has not only prepared a position and ground for us to be saved but also provided a position and ground for us to be saved *to the uttermost.* We are well able hereafter to live differently from the manner that we now live. Let us say Hallelujah, because today there is a gospel of glad tidings for saints as well as for sinners.

The Christian Life As Ordained by God

What kind of life should a Christian live according to God's will? This does not refer to a matured Christian, but to each and every born-again believer. By knowing the kind of life one ought to live, he can realize his great lack. Let us look at several passages of Scripture which describe the various facets of this life.

(1) A Life That Is Free from Sins. "She shall bring forth a son; and thou shalt call his name Jesus; for it is he that shall save his people from their sins" (Matt. 1.21). At both Chefoo and Peking, some brothers said to me, "We liked to call Him Christ

before, but henceforth we will say Jesus, our Savior." Why is He called Jesus? It is because this name means "he shall save his people from their sins."

You have accepted Jesus as your Savior, and you have received the grace of forgiveness. All this is true, for which you can thank and praise God. But what has Jesus done for you after all? "He shall save his people from their sins." This is ordained by God and accomplished by Jesus. The question now is, are you still living in sins or have you come out of sins? Does your old temper continue to flare up; do your old thoughts continue to trouble you; and has your pride or selfishness remained unchanged? In other words, are you still bound by your sins? Or have you come out completely from them?

I have used the following illustration many times before, but I will use it here once more. A life jacket is different from a lifeboat. When a person falls into the sea, he grasps the life jacket thrown to him. Thus he does not sink; yet he does not get out of the water either. He stays in a condition of neither living nor dying. A lifeboat, though, is something quite different. The person who has fallen into the sea can be drawn out of the water and put into a lifeboat. Similarly speaking, the salvation of our Lord cannot be likened to that of a life jacket but to that of a lifeboat. The Lord will not let you remain in a state of "neither living nor dying"; He will instead save His people from their sins because He has not left us in sins. Hence the salvation spoken of in the Bible is a saving us from sins. Nevertheless, how many of us, though truly still saved, continue to live in sins! Can the Bible be untrue? Certainly not. The Bible is right, whereas our *experience* is wrong.

(2) *A Life That Holds Intimate Communion with God.* "And hath raised up a horn of salvation for us in the house of his servant David . . . that we being delivered out of the hand of our enemies should serve him without fear, in holiness and righteousness

before him all our days" (Luke 1.69, 74–75). God has raised up "a horn of salvation" in the house of David. This horn of salvation we have already possessed. What does this do for us, and to what extent has He delivered us? He has delivered us "out of the hand of our enemies." How then should we live today now that we are delivered out of the enemies' hands? Is it that we should *sometimes* serve Him in righteousness and holiness? Thank and praise the Lord, He wants us to serve Him "in holiness and righteousness *all our days.*" As long as we shall live, we are to serve Him in holiness and righteousness. Such is the life ordained by God.

Yet we have to shamefully acknowledge that though we have been delivered by God from the hands of our enemies, we have not served Him in holiness and righteousness all our days. If the word in the Scriptures be true, then our personal experience must be wrong.

(3) A Life That Is Wholly Satisfied with the Lord. "Whosoever drinketh of the water that I shall give him shall never thirst; but the water that I shall give him shall become in him a well of water springing up unto eternal life" (John 4.14). How precious is this word! Our Lord does not say that a *special* Christian will receive from Him a *special* grace so that in him there will be a well of water springing up to eternal life. Not at all. Our Lord says, *"whosoever"*! Moreover, He addresses this word directly to a Samaritan woman—a complete stranger! He says to her, If you believe, you will have this living water, which will then become a well of water springing up to eternal life.

What is thirst? It is a being unsatisfied. But whoever drinks the water offered by the Lord shall never thirst again. *Every* Christian may know not only contentment but even eternal satisfaction. If he knows only contentment, he has yet to know more. What God has given causes us to be satisfied forever.

Many times when you walk the city's main street, are you

thirsty? When you walk by department stores such as Wing On and Sincere,* are you thirsting after something? You perhaps figure if you could have this or that, how good life would be. This is thirst. When you notice what your schoolmate or colleague has, do you thirst for what he possesses? Yet our Lord declares, "Whosoever drinketh of the water that I shall give him shall never thirst; but the water that I shall give him shall become in him a well of water springing up unto eternal life." Such is the kind of life He gives, even though our experience tells a different story.

Our Lord Jesus says that having Him is enough, but we say having Him is still not enough—we want still other things to satisfy us. Which is in error—what the Lord gives or what we experience? One of these two *must* be wrong. Yet the Lord never writes a check with insufficient funds to back it up. He gives whatever He says He gives. Our experience in the past is like being "half-saved." Why does He say that whoever believes in Him shall never thirst? Because something new has happened in that person. Within him there is now a new desire and a new satisfaction.

Let me ask you this: Do you live before God serving Him daily in holiness and righteousness? Is there something springing forth from you that can quench the thirst of other people? The Chinese have a saying—"Nothing doing"; but we Christians can say, "Nothing asking." We ask for nothing else because we are fully satisfied with the Lord himself. Is this true of you? If you still feel unsatisfied, your life experience is doubtlessly wrong.

(4) A Life That Is Full of Influence. "Jesus stood and cried, saying, If any man thirst, let him come unto me and drink. He that believeth on me, as the scripture hath said, from within him shall flow rivers of living water" (John 7.37-38). From whose innermost being shall flow rivers of living water? Not just from those

---

*Two large department stores then in Shanghai.—*Translator*

so-called *special* Christians — such as the apostles Paul, Peter and John; but also from whoever believes — such as from within you and me. This causes people in contact with us to find satisfaction and to be thirsty no more.

I have a friend by whose presence when contact is made with her you are immediately convicted of the vulgarity of loving the world, the foolishness of being ambitious, and the tastelessness of coveting. One day you may consider a certain matter quite unsatisfactory, but as you touch her, you sense you are already satisfied by the Lord. Or you may one day find satisfaction in a certain thing, yet a touch with her makes you feel that that thing is really quite nothing. Out of the believer, says Jesus, shall flow rivers of living water. This is what our Lord has provided, and it should be the common experience of *all* Christians. For what I say here is not to be merely the experience of special saints, but the experience all Christians ought to have in common.

We need to inquire of ourselves, do people have no more thirst once they have had contact with us? Or do they continue to feel thirsty after they have been with us? If when people say their life is miserable, sad and undone, we in response acknowledge the same thing, then this shows we are not rivers of living water but are barren deserts which dry up the moisture and deaden the plants. Such a condition proves we are wrong. Yet God is never wrong.

(5) A Life That Is Free from the Power of Sin. "Unto you first God, having raised up his Servant, sent him to bless you, in turning away every one of you from your iniquities" (Acts 3.26). This is the message Peter delivered at the porch of the temple in Jerusalem. What the Lord Jesus has accomplished is in turning people from their iniquities. The *minimum* experience of a Christian is to be freed from sin. Whatever he knows to be sin must be overcome. I do not insist we must conquer the sins which we have no knowledge of, but I do declare we ought to overcome through our Lord all sins which we *know*. We should overcome

all those which have entangled us for many years. The Bible says, "even if a man be overtaken in *any* trespass" (Gal. 6.1a); yet too often our experience as believers is that we only overcome occasionally. How abnormal is our experience!

"What shall we say then? Shall we continue in sin, that grace may abound? God forbid. We who died to sin, how shall we any longer live therein?" (Rom. 6.1-2) We who believe in the Lord Jesus have died to sin. Thus, no Christian should continue in it. How do we know we are dead to sin? Paul provides the answer in the very next verse: "Are ye ignorant that all who were baptized into Christ Jesus were baptized into his death?" (v.3) In other words, those who have been baptized are dead to sin. For baptism is into the death of Christ Jesus: "We were buried . . . with him through baptism into death: that like as Christ was raised up from the dead through the glory of the Father, so we also might walk in newness of life" (v.4). This is the kind of life a Christian should live daily. All who have been baptized ought to walk in newness of life. These are not special Christians Paul has in view here; rather, they are the *newly* baptized ones. We have all been baptized, therefore we should walk in newness of life. Such experience is ordained by God for all believers.

"Sin shall not have dominion over you: for ye are not under law, but under grace" (Rom. 6.14). Oh, how I love this verse! Let me ask you: Who is the one in view here who is not under law but under grace? Is it Andrew Murray? or Paul? or Peter or John? Or is it, that *all who believe* are not under law but under grace? How many of you are under grace today? Praise and thanks be to our God, *all* of us are under grace, with none of us still under law!

The words which precede this statement we have just discussed are, "sin shall not have dominion over you." Here it declares that sin shall not be our lord! Victory is not the experience of special Christians, it is instead an experience all believers may share; because all who are saved are under grace. When I was first saved, I considered this verse to be most precious. In those days I confessed I had many victories over many sins, and God was truly gracious to me. Yet there was one particular sin which had dominion over me, and a few other sins which frequently returned to trouble me again and again. This can be illustrated by what happened to me one day as I was walking on the street. There I met a certain brother to whom I nodded my head in acknowledgement. Shortly thereafter I came out of a store and met him a second time. And for the second time I acknowledged him by nodding my head. I entered into still another store and when I came out of it, I met him once more. So again I nodded my head. I crossed over to another street, and there to my amazement I encountered him a fourth time! Another street after that and I saw him again. Within one day and I had met him five times, and five times I had nodded my head. This can illustrate, can it not, the way in which we meet up with sin.

We do not know why we always encounter this or that particular sin as though it were following us. Yet it does. Some find ill-temper following them; some, pride following them; some, jealousy; others, laziness; still others, lying; some, misery and self-pity; some, meanness; some, selfishness; others, unclean thoughts; and still others, impure passions. In fact, everybody seems to have a special sin that always follows him or her. I myself found a few sins that followed me most powerfully and tenaciously. I had to concede that sin *did* have dominion over me. I finally confessed to the Lord, "You say that sin shall not have the rule over me; therefore, I consent that the fault must be in me and not in Your word."

Although you may live a defeated life, you nonetheless know that this is not the life ordained by God. If sin still has the rule over you, you should clearly understand that this is not what God has ordained. For His word plainly says, "sin shall not have dominion over you."

"There is therefore now no condemnation to them that are in Christ Jesus" (Rom. 8.1). In my preaching I have explained the word "condemnation" many times. Some twenty years ago, from an old manuscript excavated from the ground, it was explained that this word in the original Greek language had two usages: one, civil; the other, legal (and thus in this latter sense, the English word "condemnation" is used). According to civil usage, it could be translated as "without strength." Hence we may legitimately retranslate this verse as follows: "There is therefore now no being without strength to them that are in Christ Jesus." How marvelous this is! Let me ask you again, whose verse is this? Only Wesley's? or Martin Luther's? or only Hudson Taylor's? What does the Scripture say here? It says that those who are in Christ Jesus are no longer without strength. Who are these people? They are all Christians — since every Christian is in Christ, and no one in Christ is without strength.

"The law of the Spirit of life in Christ Jesus made me free from the law of sin and of death" (v.2). I will repeat a hundred times that it is not those special saints who are freed from the law of sin and of death. It is instead true that *every* Christian is set free from the law of sin and of death. What is meant by being "without strength"? It is what is spoken of in Romans 7: "to will is present with me, but to do that which is good is not. For the good which I would I do not: but the evil which I would not, that I practise" (vv.18b–19). In other words, the total thrust of Romans 7 indicates that I am without strength, I cannot do it. The history of many a Christian is marked by a cycle of resolutions and broken promises. Yet we thank and praise God that His word unmistakably declares that no Christian is now without strength.

What is law? It is something which always repeats itself. A law acts the same way and produces the same result at any place and under any circumstance. It is a constant phenomenon, reveals a continuous habit, and always ends with the same effect. There is, for instance, the force of gravity at the center of the earth. Whenever you throw an object, that object is always attracted by this gravitational force and falls downward. This force of gravity is thus a universal law.

For some, then, the losing of one's temper becomes a law. He may endure temptation once or twice, but on the third occasion of being provoked he begins to be agitated, and by the fourth time he completely loses his temper. It does not matter which person or thing he encounters. At first he *can* endure a provocation, but his temper will always eventually explode later. So that with each occasion he is tempted to lose his temper, and without exception it ends up with the same result.

Pride oftentimes acts the same way. You may remain untouched at the first word with which you are praised, but you will feel your face begin to glow with pride upon hearing the second word of praise. Whatever passes through the same procedure and produces the same result constitutes a law. In short, we sin till sinning becomes a law.

It needs to be said again that it is not those special Christians who are made free from the law of sin. Rather, *every* Christian hereafter is not to be without strength; *every* Christian is now set free from the law of sin. The Scripture passages quoted above are facts, not commands. They therefore ought to be the experience of all believers. Yet how sad that our experience does not measure up to God's word.

(6) A Life That Overcomes Environment. "Who shall separate us from the love of Christ? shall tribulation, or anguish, or persecution, or famine, or nakedness, or peril, or sword? . . . Nay, in all these things we are more than conquerors through him that loved us" (Rom. 8.35, 37). Through the Lord who loves us we are made more than conquerors in all things. This is, in fact, the kind of experience a Christian should have. Yet a slight change in another's countenance—not to mention tribulation or sword!—will cause us to lose the consciousness of Christ's love. Nevertheless, Paul declared that in all these things we more than conquer.

Victory is to be the Christian's *normal* experience; defeat is abnormal. For according to God's will, every Christian should more than conquer in all kinds of environment. Whether it be tribulation or anguish or persecution or famine or nakedness or peril or sword, we shall not only conquer, but *more than* conquer! Any increase in difficulty will make no difference. The world may look upon Christians as mad. So what if we *are* deemed mad! Through the love of Christ, we will not mind these things, because we more than conquer them. And such is to be the Christian's experience as ordained by God. But what is *our* experience? Sad to say, we have not lived rightly. For with but a little tribulation which comes our way we scream and complain how we have endured and suffered. Yet if we live rightly, we shall more than conquer in all these things.

"Thanks be unto God, who always leadeth us in triumph in Christ, and maketh manifest through us the savor of his knowledge in every place" (2 Cor. 2. 14). The Christian life is not one that sometimes conquers and is sometimes defeated; is not one that is defeated in the morning and is conquering in the afternoon. It is *always* in triumph. According to the Biblical standard, it is to be deemed *strange* if you do *not* overcome and to be reckoned as *common* if you *do* overcome!

(7) A Life That Practices Good. "We are his workmanship, created in Christ Jesus for good works, which God afore prepared that we should walk in them" (Eph. 2.10). We all know that this verse continues from those very familiar and precious verses of 8 and 9. What is mentioned in the preceding verses is that we are saved by grace; but here it says we are His workmanship, created for good works which God has in advance prepared for us. This is not a description of the experience of some special Christians; it is instead the common experience shared by all believers— that is to say, God saves us *all* that we may *all* do good.

Do you do good according to what God has ordained? Or are you performing good works on the one hand and murmuring on the other? For instance, perhaps you are mopping the floor. As you are mopping, you at the same time wonder why only you and one other brother are doing this. Why are not the other brothers mopping too? As you muse, you become either proud of yourself or begin to murmur at others. This cannot be viewed as doing good works. Every Christian should do good with his heart full of joy, nothing stingy or stinting about it, nothing selfish, but a willingness to pour out one's life for other people. How sad it would be if only the best Christian could do good works.

(8) A Life That Is Full of Light. "Again therefore Jesus spake unto them, saying, I am the light of the world: he that followeth me shall not walk in the darkness, but shall have the light of life" (John 8.12). This is the life which God has ordained for Christians. It is not that a *special* class of Christians can walk in the light of life, but that *all* who follow Christ should not walk in darkness but can have the light of life. A Christian who is full of light is a *normal* Christian; the one who has no light is doubtless abnormal.

(9) A Life That Is Wholly Sanctified. "The God of peace himself sanctify you wholly: and may your spirit and soul and body be preserved entire, without blame at the coming of our Lord Jesus Christ" (1 Thess. 5.23). This is the prayer of the apostle Paul for the Thessalonian believers. Since he prayed, "sanctify you wholly," it is evident that being entirely sanctified is possible and that to "be preserved entire, without blame" is also possible. For God is able to sanctify us completely and to preserve us blameless.

All these matters which have been mentioned above pertain to what the Lord has provided for Christians. His salvation is such as to enable all believers to maintain uninterrupted communion with God as well as to overcome sin so completely that they may tread it all under their feet. This, then, is the life ordained by the Lord for us all. And this is no theory but is very much a fact.

Must Experience God's Full Salvation

What is your experience today? If your experience is different from that spelled out in the Scriptures, then you are in need of *full* salvation. Your being saved is a fact; but you have not obtained salvation in fullness. May I therefore bring you glad tidings? What the Lord Jesus has accomplished on the cross not only can save you from the penalty of sin but can also deliver you from the pain of sin. For He has prepared such a full salvation for us that we may daily live in victory as well as receive the initial salvation.

What is victory? Victory is actually a remedial facet to salvation. This is so because at the time of our being saved, something was missing—yet not on God's part; for He never gives us a salvation which lets us live a wandering life: He wants us to have *full* salvation. But because we are not well saved, we today need such a remedial facet, which is none other than the experience of victory.

Would God save us and let us live on continually sinning and repenting? Can we continue in sin, having had the Son of God die for us? Is it possible that because we sinned before we were saved we cannot help but sin afterwards? Shall sin have dominion over us even after we are saved? How opposite both sin and God are to each other. Would God therefore allow sin to remain in us? Never. It is most hateful! Whether it is physical, psychological or dispositional, sin is still sin.

Let us say to the Lord, "Lord, I praise and thank You, because what You have accomplished on the cross has delivered me from the power of sin as well as saved me from its penalty. Let me see my lack and cause me to seek for victory." If our experience does not agree with what the Scripture declares, then we are surely in need of victory. May the Lord enlighten us that we may know ourselves. May we not deceive ourselves, imagining that sinning is inevitable for a Christian. I think no thought hurts our Lord more than this kind of attitude.

What do we *really* think the cross of Christ has accomplished? Has it accomplished only a little for us? Let us not lie to ourselves. Let us not boast that we can suppress and control ourselves. For such suppression and control of ourselves do not constitute victory. The victory of Christ is to destroy sin completely. And praise the Lord that sin has been trodden under His feet. But today those of us who have neither obtained uninterrupted communion with God nor had the power to overcome sin are in need of victory. May God be gracious to each one of us.

3 | The Nature of the Life That Wins

"The Strength of Israel [margin, "the Victory of Israel"] will not lie nor repent; for he is not a man, that he should repent" (1 Sam. 15.29).

The first mention of victory in the whole Bible is found in 1 Samuel 15.29. There it says that Victory will not lie nor repent. The Victory of Israel is neither an experience nor an event; it is a Person. I am sure we all know who that Person is. It is Christ! Hence let me tell you today that victory does not reside in ourselves, nor is it our own experience. Victory is not you as the problem; victory is the person of Christ living for you! And thus the victory we obtain will neither lie nor repent. Praise God, victory is a living Person!

According to the word of God, the nature of victorious life is many-sided. But we shall only describe five of its many characteristics.

The Meaning of This Life—Not a Changed Life, but an Exchanged One

First of all, please notice that victory is an exchanged life, not a changed life. Victory is not that I have changed, but rather that I have been *exchanged*. One verse which is most familiar to us is Galatians 2.20: "I have been crucified with Christ; and it is no longer I that live, but Christ liveth in me: and that life which I now live in the flesh I live in faith, the faith which is in the

Son of God." What is meant by this verse? It has only one meaning: the life spoken of is an exchanged life. Basically, it is no longer I, for it has absolutely nothing to do with me. It is not that the bad I has become the good I, or the unclean I has changed to be the clean I. It is simply "not I." Today people make a serious mistake in thinking that victory is progressive and defeat is retrogressive—that if a person is able to control his temper or maintain an intimate fellowship with God, then he is victorious. Not so. Let us ever keep in mind that victory has basically no relation to one's own self.

One brother confessed with crying that he could not overcome. I frankly told him that he indeed could not overcome. He continued to say he could not overcome. How could I help him? I said to this brother: "God has never demanded that *you* overcome. He has never asked you to change your bad temper to a good temper, your hardness to gentleness, or your sorrow to joy. The way of God is simply to exchange your life for Another Life, which therefore has absolutely nothing to do with you."

A sister complained that it appeared easy for others to overcome, but it was very difficult for her to do so. Because her temper was worse than other people's, because her thoughts were dirtier, and her disposition was more artful than most, therefore, she explained, she just could not control herself. My answer to her was this, "In truth, it is not only *hard* for you to overcome, it is *so* hard that it is *impossible* for you to do so. Do you really think it would be much easier to overcome if you by nature were a little more honest, a little better in temper, and a little cleaner in thought? Let me tell you, there is no such thing, because no matter how gentle and holy and perfect a person is, he cannot overcome unless he as a person is removed and lets Christ move in. Similarly, a person who is even worse and dirtier and more defective can experience victory only when he too as a person has moved out and has let Christ move in. Inasmuch as the one who is of a good temper and is moral needs to believe in the Lord Jesus for salvation as much as does the person whose temper is bad and whose morals are utterly corrupt, so the good-tempered and morally better needs victory for sanctification just as much as does the ill-tempered and morally corrupt. Victory is Christ himself, it has nothing to do with you and me."

Once I met a sister whom I considered to be the most difficult among sisters to find victory. It required two hours for her to relate to me her defeats and failures from childhood till fifty years of age. She had no way to overcome her pride and ill-temper. She suffered defeats all the time. I had never met a person who desired victory as much as she, nor had I seen anyone who found victory so elusive as she. She moaned over her failures. She even thought of suicide because of her defeats. She found herself so helpless. As she was relating her story to me, I began to laugh. "Today," I said, "the Lord Jesus has met an ideal patient whom He can heal!"

This sister was so full of the sense of her own sins—pride and ill-temper—that she would surely contaminate you by what she told you if you did not know what victory is. You would probably agree with her that there was no hope. But from God's word there come glad tidings of great joy—because though you cannot change, you may nevertheless be exchanged! The life that wins is an exchanged life. If it were up to you, you would never make it; but if it is a matter of Christ, there is absolutely no problem. The question is: who overcomes, you or Christ? If it is Christ, then it does not matter, how you by nature are, even though you may be ten times worse than others.

I ask you, what is victory? It is not *you* overcoming, it is *Christ* who overcomes for you. The Scriptures teach only one kind of victory, and this is what Galatians 2.20 declares: "it is no longer I that live, but Christ liveth in me." The Fukienese in South China have a saying, "No change even with death." I told this to the brethren in Peking and observed that we should all say to ourselves, "No change even with death." Praise to the Lord that I have not changed, but I *have been exchanged!*

One sister asked me what the difference was between changed

and exchanged. I used the following illustration. Suppose I held in my hand a copy of an old worn-out Bible. If I wanted to change it, I would add a new cover, apply some glue, and imprint upon the cover in gold the letters spelling "Holy Bible." Furthermore, if any letter within its pages was missing, I would print it with ink; or if a letter was not clear, I would ink it more plainly with a pen. I did not know how long this process would take me, nor was I certain if it would come out well. If, however, I decided to exchange it for a new Bible, this could be done in a matter of a second. And in that case, I could give my worn-out copy to a bookseller and he would exchange it for a new Bible. It is just the same in our spiritual life. Since God has given His Son to you, you need not spend any strength of yours but simply give Him your worn-out life in exchange for His Son's life.

Let me use another illustration. Several years ago I bought a watch with a guarantee on it of two years. But as it turned out this watch was in my house for far less time than it was at the company's premises; for it began to run inaccurately after a while. As a result, it had to be taken to the company many times for repair—once, twice, even ten times. I was tired of running it over there, and moreover, the watch remained inaccurate. Hence I requested the company to exchange it for another watch. They replied, however, that they could not do so because there was no such company regulation that allowed for this. But since they guaranteed the watch for two years, they told me they would continue to repair it within the guarantee period. This went on for eight months, yet the company still refused to exchange it for a good watch. Finally, I grew so tired of this that I left my watch at the company permanently. This illustration can serve to show that man's way is always one of repairing. Repair, repair, and repair again within the guarantee period of life. Man has no way for exchange.

Even in the Old Testament time of Bible history we find that God's way was never to repair, nor to change, but to *exchange*. Note this passage, for example: "to appoint unto them that mourn in Zion, to give unto them a garland for ashes, the oil of joy for mourning, the garment of praise for the spirit of heaviness; that they may be called trees of righteousness, the planting of Jehovah, that he may be glorified" (Is. 61.3). To *substitute* is God's way. He does not change ashes but instead gives a garland for ashes. Neither does He change sorrow in the slightest; He instead gives the oil of gladness for sorrow. Nor does He change the heaviness into praise, but gives the garment of praise in exchange for the spirit of heaviness. "Change" is never God's way; His way is always "*ex*change."

All these years I have not been able to change myself, yet God has exchanged me. This is holiness, this is perfection, this is victory, and this is the life of God's Son! Hallelujah! Henceforth the gentleness of Christ is my gentleness: the holiness of Christ is my holiness: the prayer life of Christ is my prayer life: the communion of Christ with God is now my communion with God. No sin is too big that I cannot overcome. No temptation is too severe that I cannot prevail. For the life that wins is Christ, not I. Will Christ ever be fearful of a big sin? Will He be afraid of great temptation? Praise God, I no longer fear because hereafter it is Christ and not I.

The Principle of This Life — a Gift, Not a Reward

There is one thing we must understand in all this, which is, that victory is a gift and not a reward. What is a gift? It is something which is freely given to you. That which you earn through work is a reward. A gift, on the other hand, asks for no effort on your part. It is that which is given gratuitously with no requirement placed upon the receiver, whereas a reward demands that someone work for it. The life that wins which we talk about does not require any effort of yours: "thanks be to God, who giveth us the victory through our Lord Jesus Christ" (1 Cor. 15.57). Victory is something which God has prepared to give to us. Our victory is obtained freely, not attained through self-effort.

Too often we believers have a serious misconception — imagining that while salvation comes to us freely, victory depends on ourselves. We know we cannot add any merit or work of ours to obtain salvation. We must simply come to the cross and accept the Lord Jesus as our Savior. This is the gospel! We realize we cannot be saved by works, yet we reason that for sanctification we must do good works after we are saved. This is to say that though you cannot be saved by works, you need to depend on works for victory.

Let me tell you that just as you are not *saved* by works, so you do not *overcome* by works. God has declared that you are unable to do good. Christ has died for you on the cross, and He is now living for you within. That which is of the flesh is flesh, and God rejects all that came from it. Nevertheless, we usually surmise that while salvation is dependent upon the substitutionary death of Christ on the cross, we should think of doing good, should do good, and expect to do good for victory in our lives. Let us realize, though, that we can do *no* good. Victory is freely given us by God!

The verse preceding 1 Corinthians 15.57 speaks of sin and death, followed by this verse which speaks of the victory God has given us. Victory means to be triumphant over death as well as law and sin. For the redemption which God has accomplished overcomes not only sin but also law, not only law but also death. How I wish I could walk among you and tell each of you in turn that there is a gospel whereby God gives victory to everyone.

You are no doubt thinking, how can I overcome temptation? How can I overcome my pride? How can I overcome my jealousy? Oh, how much effort you have spent, and yet how many times you end up in despair. But I have a gospel to present to you today, which is this: that the gentleness, the holiness, the prayer life, and all that is in the Lord Jesus are given to you freely. As you receive Him, His all is yours. And if that is not glad tidings, then what is?

Calculate, if you will, how much time and strength you must

spend in order to always pray and to maintain uninterrupted communion with God. Reflect on how much effort you must exert to overcome sins and ill-temper. You may be able to confess your sins, but you are unable to refrain from sinning. You frequently lie, and in spite of your exertion against it you continue to lie. I have met a number of brothers and sisters who told me that though they tried not to lie, they could not change themselves to keep from lying. I have a gospel of glad tidings for you indeed today! God has freely given to you the holiness, the patience, the perfection, the love, and the faithfulness of the Lord Jesus. He freely gives to everyone who desires it. God gives to you intimate communion with himself and holy living and perfect beauty such as is found in Christ. This is all a gift. But if you fancy to overcome by yourself, you will not be able to change your ill-temper or pride even after twenty years of effort. You will remain the same as you were twenty years before.

Nevertheless, God has here a perfect salvation for you. He makes the patience of Christ to be your patience, the holiness of Christ to be your holiness, the communion of Christ to be your communion, and all the virtues of Christ to be your virtues. Hallelujah! Such is the salvation which God has provided us. This is what He will freely give to us!

Have you ever observed a sinner who tried to save himself by works? I have encountered quite a few of them. When you meet such a sinner, will you not tell him he need not do anything because Christ has already done all? Since God has given the Lord Jesus to him, all he needs to do is to accept Him. In like manner with respect to victory, today I would deliver a similar message to you — you do not need to do *anything,* since Christ has done it all. God has given the Lord Jesus to you, and it is well if you receive Him. The victory is yours. As salvation is obtained through God's free grace without your works, so victory over sin is God's free gift without your works too. Salvation needs no effort of yours, and victory does not require your effort either.

I have here a Bible. Suppose I want to give it to you. The

words written within are not your writing, the cover was not put on by you, neither have you imprinted the title with gold letters. All these were done by others. It is to be given to you as a gift. In the same way is this matter of victory, for it is a gift God freely gives to you. We are not to proceed gradually to victory, holiness, and perfection by our own effort and works. No, no, no! If there is anyone who has overcome, his victory must have come from the Lord Jesus.

Recently I met a sister who told me that having spent twenty years in trying to overcome her pride and ill-temper she had not only failed but also felt quite hopeless. This was what I said to her in response: "If you expect to overcome your pride and ill-temper by your own effort, you will not succeed even after twenty more years. But you can be freed from sins today if you simply accept the gift of God. This gift is freely given by Him, and it is yours by accepting it. The Lord Jesus is the victory. And by accepting Him as your victory, you obtain the victory." Whereupon she accepted this gift that God had given her. Do realize today the vanity of your works and the failure of your life. Accept the Lord Jesus Christ and you shall overcome.

There is one verse with which we are all familiar: "sin shall not have dominion over you: for ye are not under law, but under grace" (Rom. 6.14). How is it that sin shall not have dominion over you? Because you are not under law but under grace. What is meant by being under law? I have mentioned many times before that being under law signifies God requiring man to work for Him. What, then, is being under grace? It denotes God working for man. If we work for God, sin shall reign over us. The wages of our works is having sin rule over us. But if God works for us, sin shall not have dominion over us. Under law, we work. Under grace, God works. When God works, sin shall not rule over us. For it is He who works, and *this* is victory. Whatever requires effort on our part is not victory. Victory comes freely to us.

Suppose there is a person who has sinned so much until sin

ning becomes wearisome and meaningless and un-Christianlike. Let me tell you that if you accept this gift of God now, you may immediately become a victorious person. For the principle of victory is the principle of gift, not of reward. And all shall be well by accepting this gift.

The Way to This Life—Obtained, Not Attained

The life that wins is to be *obtained,* never to be *attained.* Obtained simply means gaining possession of a thing. Attained, on the other hand, implies you have a long way to go and that you will proceed slowly without the assurance of arriving at the goal someday. Yet the victory of a Christian is not attained through a slow process. Once I was climbing Mount Kuling. Brother Sing-Liang Yu invited me to go with him. As we gradually climbed, I felt increasingly tired. After we had covered some distance, I asked brother Yu how much farther we had to go. He replied that it was not very far to the top. So we continued to trod on slowly. Still we had not arrived. Whenever I asked brother Yu, I always got the answer that we were almost there. Finally we did arrive. But suppose I were to go up the mountain by being carried in a sedan chair; in that case I would have *obtained* Kuling, not *attained* it. All things pertaining to the Holy Spirit are obtained. So that all which is related to victory must be received.

"If, by the trespass of the one, death reigned through the one; much more shall they that receive the abundance of grace and of the gift of righteousness reign in life through the one, even Jesus Christ" (Rom. 5.17). Here God declares that victory is a gift for you to accept. Victory is not something for you to slowly attain. It is a gift given you; it demands no work of yours. Suppose I give my Bible to you. Do you need to exert effort to get it? Just stretch out your arm and you have it in a second. It being a gift to you, you need not go home and fast for it, neither must you kneel towards Jerusalem three times a day, nor are you obligated to resolve that you will not lose your temper hereafter.

No, all you need to do is to receive it. So how many procedures must you go through to receive this Bible? There is no procedure but to take it with your hand. The same is it with victory; it is a gift that you obtain, not attain.

We are familiar with 1 Corinthians 1.30 which says that of God are we "in Christ Jesus, who was made unto us wisdom from God, both righteousness and sanctification and redemption" (mg.). Since wisdom is the overall subject here, we can leave it without commenting on it. Here we find that God has made Christ to be three things to us: righteousness, sanctification, redemption. Now let me ask you, when did God make Christ our righteousness? You will all correctly reply that it was when Christ died on the cross and when you received Him as your righteousness. You did not need to weep three days before you received Him as your righteousness, nor did you need to apologize to people whom you had offended before you possessed Him. Praise to the Lord that the Son of God has died for you; therefore, the moment you believed you obtained this righteousness. Yet sadly, in the matter of accepting the Lord Jesus as sanctification, you circle around yourself, wasting your energy. Just as you instantly obtained righteousness when you accepted the Lord as your righteousness, so you may immediately obtain sanctification the moment you receive Him as your sanctification. If you are planning to walk slowly on the Christian path with the expectation that one day you may attain sanctification, you will never get there. Whoever thinks of accomplishing his own righteousness will not be saved; but by the same token, whoever thinks of achieving his own sanctification will never gain victory.

What is the difference between "obtain" and "attain"? An important element in the difference is time. One is something instantaneous while the other is something gradual. There was a story about a chicken thief. He usually stole seven chickens a week. Later on he thought of reforming himself. So he began to steal one chicken less each week so that after six weeks he would stop stealing altogether. That may be true of chicken thieves, but the victory of the Lord is obtained instantly.

When I was in Chefoo, I met a brother whose temper was terrible. When it flared up, his entire household was frightened. His wife, his children, his employees in his embroidery shop, and even the Christian brethren were in fear and trembling. This latter circumstance was because sometimes he would cause disturbances even in the meeting place. One day he confessed to me that he had no way to control his temper. I told him that if he accepted the Lord as his victory, he could obtain victory immediately. Whereupon he accepted, and he experienced victory.

Some time after that he asked me how many days it had been since he had obtained the victory. We together figured it had been about a month. He then related to me that one day during that period his wife was so ill that it appeared she was about to die. Had such a thing happened before, he would have been so anxious that he would have walked from one room to another with a long face and a developing bad temper. But this time, when his wife was ill and her pulse grew weak, he softly said to God that it was well even if He should take her. His bad temper totally disappeared. His wife got better and was treated with acupuncture. Moreover, he was now taking care of his wife with patient love!

On the day I left Chefoo, he came to see me off. He told me that within the last twenty-four hours, he had had no anxiety whatsoever, as though it were some other person's wife and not his own who was still ill. At this time as well, his women employees were very difficult to handle. He told me that during the last month many things had happened at his shop. Formerly he would have been very angry, but now he took them as not being his own problems. He could even laughingly ask why they did such things. His ill-temper was gone. I tell you, this is *ob*tainment. Had it been *at*tainment, this brother would not have been able to achieve victory even after twenty years' effort.

Once a missionary went to India. She brought nothing but her bad disposition with her. She often lost her temper. She herself once confessed that if *she* could be patient, *the whole world* could be patient! Her spiritual companion had already obtained the secret of taking Christ as the life that wins. She wrote and told this missionary lady about the secret of victory and how it was to be obtained. As soon as the letter was received, this missionary acted according to what the letter said. Three months later, the missionary's companion received her reply. This was the gist of her reply: "As soon as I read your letter, I knew that here were the glad tidings! Christ is patience. The moment I accepted Him, my bad temper disappeared. But due to the seriousness of my last most recent failures, I knew I dared not speak out till I had tested if for three months. Those Indian servants of mine are slow, but very sly. And in the past, each time when I would close the door, I would slam it to show my displeasure with them. However, ever since I began to practice that which you suggested in your letter, I have not slammed the door once, neither have I had the attitude of being displeased anymore." Surely, victory over sin is fully accomplished by the Lord for you; therefore, you do not need to exert any effort.

Let me repeat that victory is something to be obtained, not to be attained.

Possessing This Life Is a Miracle

"Work out your own salvation . . .; for it is God who worketh in you both to will and to work, for his good pleasure" (Phil. 2.12b-13). Thus has Paul reminded us. The reason why we can "work out" according to God's "good pleasure" is simply because it is He who enables us to so work out. It is God who moves within us to be holy. It is not because we have exercised great strength, but entirely because God works all in us. For this holy and perfect life is not the result of our effort but the accomplished work of the Lord himself.

I readily acknowledge that unless there is a miracle, many people on earth will never be able to get rid of their corruption. Some people do not know their failures; they do not see their inability. Other people realize that they have no control over their pride or disposition or temper. Unless there is a miracle, none will come into victory. For who among us can overcome sin? The human way is to suppress sin. But when God does the work, He miraculously removes our old man and gives us a pure heart. Were we to know the victory of God, how happy we would be!

There was a sister whose temper was fiercer than most people's. Her husband, her children, and nearly everybody else were afraid of her. But she was a Christian. What could she do with her fierce temper? After many years, she came to accept the Lord Jesus as her victory. Yet immediately upon doing so she was confronted with a serious test. She had accepted the Lord Jesus as her victory the previous day, and the next morning while she was combing her hair and before she came downstairs she met the trial. Her husband and a servant were trying to hang a crystal lamp downstairs. This crystal lamp was worth quite a lot. Somehow her husband and the servant, through carelessness, dropped the lamp and it was shattered. Just then she came downstairs. When the husband saw her, he was stunned for fear that there would be a big explosion of her temper. Contrary to all expectations, though, she quietly said that since the lamp was broken, it should be swept up. Her husband was astonished. Ordinarily she would quarrel over a little cup or plate being broken. Today she should have truly exploded. Confronted by such a change, he asked her whether she had slept well that night or was she sick? Her answer was that she was not sick, only that the Lord had miraculously taken her old man away. Her husband cried out, "This is a miracle, this is a miracle!" It was a miracle indeed. Praise God.

Mr. Charles G. Trumbull, in his day the editor in America of the *Sunday School Times,* was quite spiritual. He acknowledged that this life that wins is truly a miracle. Once he testified to a church elder that after he had accepted the Lord Jesus as his life, he had not once lost his temper, neither did he have any inclination to do so. "Do you mean to say that the old sins have all been eliminated?" asked the elder. "Indeed," replied Mr. Trumbull. "Well, I believe this is true in *your* life because I believe your word," said the elder, "but this will never be factual for me." Later on, Mr. Trumbull asked the elder to pray with him. That day they had a long prayer session. The elder finally accepted the fact as accomplished. One day Mr. Trumbull met the elder, who testified, saying, "Never in my life have I experienced anything like what happened that evening with you in prayer. It is truly a miracle! There is no need to struggle, to exert strength, nor even to desire it. This is really marvelous, it *is* a miracle." Sometime afterwards, he wrote to Mr. Trumbull saying that in the place where he worked, there was some evil influence among the members of the Board of Trustees. Yet, whereas in the past he had had to suppress himself, now he did not even have a heart of agitation. What a miracle this was!

Do you have any problem you cannot solve or any sin you cannot deal with? If so, the Lord Jesus can perform a miracle for you immediately. Whatever has frustrated you for years He can solve at once. The Lord will work a miracle for you irrespective of what your sin is, be it of the spirit, of the flesh, of thought, of body, of disposition, of inability to do God's will, of lack of consecration, or inability to confess. You are not able to consecrate yourself, but He can cause you to do so; you cannot be patient, but He will make you patient. He is well able to overcome every sin. God is able. All is well with His miracle of grace!

The Consequence — an Expressed Life, Not a Suppressed One

The consequence of having this life that wins is seen in an expressed, not a suppressed, life. *Our* so-called victories are always done through suppression. One old lady held in her temper whenever she met unpleasant things. Outwardly she wore a smil ing face, but inwardly she was controlling her feelings with great difficulty. After living such a suppressed life for some time, she found the pressure within her had so built up that she began to spit blood. And why? Simply because the problem had remained with her. Yet true victory in the Christian's walk is an *expressed* life, not a suppressed one. An expressed life signifies a showing forth that which has already been obtained. It is what Philippians 2.12 intimates to us, when it declares for us to "work *out* [our] own salvation." Previously we tried hard to cover ourselves; now we dare to express the victory of Christ in us. Formerly, the more suppressed the better; today, the more expressed the better. Since Christ lives in me, I want to express Him before the world.

Mrs. Jessie Penn-Lewis had a young girl friend who knew how to compose poems and who was skillful in leading children into this victorious life. One day Mrs. Penn-Lewis paid her a special visit in order to see how she helped the children. On that particular day, this young friend invited more than ten children to a meal. When they had just finished eating and before the table was cleaned, a guest suddenly arrived. She asked these children what should be done to the dirty table. They suggested covering it up with a clean table cloth. She complied by doing just that. After the guest was gone, she asked the children whether or not the guest had seen the spills and stains on the table. They answered no. Then she challenged the children by asking: "Although the guest did not see these spills and stains, would you say that the table is clean?" Their reply was this: "Even though the guest did not see anything, the dirty table is still dirty."

Let me say right here that many people are ready to be clean outside but not to be clean inside. Who dares to reveal the thoughts and feelings of his or her heart? And yet we consider ourselves to be victorious. When people praise us, we try to look humble. We may appear to be patient, but we hide our impatience under cover. Allow me to speak frankly, that whatever is suppressed within is *not* victory. Only when you and I go out and Christ comes in do we have victory. And in that case, whatever is expressible is victory.

A sister I know easily lost her temper. One day her maid broke a vase. The sister quickly covered herself with a blanket, pretending to sleep. She was fearful lest she would see the scene and explode. This is a suppressed life.

Suppose a fruit peddler came by and asked you to purchase some fruit from him, but you sent him away without buying any fruit. And suppose he came the second and the third time, but you still did not buy from him. In order to sell his fruits, he had to suppress his resentment each time you failed to buy any of his produce. This is not victory, it is but a business policy. The victory of Christ, though, purifies even the heart. In short, victory means a pure heart.

A brother recently crossed the threshold of victory. He was already over fifty, and he had studied the classics of Confucius all his life. Though he had believed in the Lord for three years, he trusted only in the shed blood of the Lord and its atoning value. During that time he did not see any major difference between Christianity and Confucianism. A follower of Confucius attempts to improve himself by works of endurance and self-control. If he is successful in such works, he becomes a sage. So that after his becoming a Christian, this brother still exercised himself in such attempts. He continued to assume the Confucian attitude of reducing a big problem to being a small matter, and of reducing a small matter to being no matter at all. But at the end of those three years he testified that he knew Christ's victory had had no touch upon his life whatsoever. How vastly different is Christianity from other religions. It is not only the difference as witnessed by the cross, it is also the difference of our having a living Christ within us. We preach the gospel of redemption, especially a Christ who lives within. Previously this brother had been a genuine disciple of Confucius by keeping a tight control over himself. Now, though, he had let go of himself and had allowed Christ to live through him — without suppression and without defeat.

The above five points reveal the nature of this life that wins. But I would add a few more words by way of conclusion. Do remember that, like salvation, victory has a date of registration. You are saved on a certain day of a certain month in a certain year (though I recognize that some people have either forgotten the date or are unaware of it). You should also record the day of the month of the year you enter into victory. For victory is a crisis, a threshold you must cross over. It should be either yea or nay. There is no almost. None can be *almost* saved. If a person is saved, he is saved! Likewise, none can *almost* overcome. Victory is victory, period! To almost overcome is in reality to *fail* to overcome. Therefore, all of us must cross this threshold of victory.

4 | How to Enter into This Life That Wins

> I have been crucified with Christ; and it is no longer I that live, but Christ liveth in me: and that life which I now live in the flesh I live in faith, the faith which is in the Son of God. (Gal. 2.20)

Having seen the kind of life ordained by God as well as the life we actually live, the way of victory according to God as well as the way according to man, together with the genuineness and nature of the life that wins, we will now learn how we enter into this victorious life. And a most important question naturally arises here: how can we obtain Christ as Victory?

The verse just quoted above shows us how to enter in. Let us first discuss the words, "it is no longer I that live, but Christ liveth in me"; because such is the life we ought to enter into. Negatively, we may say "it is no longer I that live." Positively, we may say that "Christ liveth in me." In Paul's letter to the Galatians, he testified that he had already arrived at this place, he had already possessed this experience, and he had already entered in. Let us observe how he arrived, possessed and entered. For the way Paul entered in is the way we also will enter in. The way he entered in is revealed by the clause preceding and the clause succeeding the words, "it is no longer I that live, but Christ liveth in me." The first condition to entering in is spelled out by these words: "I have been crucified with Christ"; and the second condition to entering in is found as follows: "and that life which I now live in the flesh I live in faith, the faith which is in the Son of God." By fulfilling these two conditions in his life Paul obtained Christ as his victory—as his righteousness, sanctification and redemption. Let us take a closer look at these two conditions.

A. Yielding—"I have been crucified with Christ"

The first condition is, "I have been crucified with Christ." Now what does this mean? Why must I be crucified with Christ before I can obtain this life that wins? Here I would ask this question: How many persons today live in us as Christians? We confess that as soon as we believe in the Lord Jesus, He comes to live in us. "Know ye not as to your own selves, that Jesus Christ is in you? unless indeed ye be reprobate" (2 Cor. 13.5). As those who have believed, we know we are not reprobates; therefore, the Lord living in us is a sure fact. However, it is tragically true that although Christ lives in us, we ourselves live in us too. In order to have Christ as our life that wins, we ourselves must move out and let go. And with ourselves moving out, we may obtain this victorious life.

Yesterday a sister asked me how she could possess this life that wins. My answer to her was quite simple: "Just move yourself away." Suppose there are two families living under one roof, and a problem arises between the two. The situation would doubtless change were the difficult family to move away. The issue today is not whether you have Christ in you, since the moment you believed, Christ indeed came to live in you. No, the issue is that you must move away. As soon as you, the sinful, move away from living together with Him who is sinless, everything will be fine. Hence, the first condition is that you must move out.

"I have been crucified with Christ." Thus declares the word of God. But what do we say about this word? Do we not say that many times we try to move out without success? We pretend to die, yet we do not die. We frequently attempt suicide, yet we still live. Too often we appear dead, yet we are not dead. We attempt to crucify ourselves, but we fail to die. What, then, is the trouble? Let us inquire into this matter more thoroughly.

(1) I Cannot

I assume we have all seen the fact of the cross. We know that when the Lord was crucified for us, He not only bore our sins but also took us with Him to the cross. We have known the teaching of Romans 6 for many years. Our old man was crucified with Him, just as our sins were borne by Him on the cross. Hence we have the knowledge that we were crucified with Christ as well as that the sin problem was solved. This is what we have emphasized throughout these years. No doubt I was crucified with Christ, but why do I not experience the effect of this co-crucifixion? The Lord has taken me to the cross, yet I remain the same. I am still bound, weak, defeated and without strength. The Scripture says, "I have been crucified with Christ." Why then am I yet powerless? Many saved Christians are working hard for this, with the vain hope of victory someday. Nevertheless, victory is far away from them.

May I say that knowing the salvation the Lord Jesus has accomplished for us is one thing, but our accepting this salvation is quite another — just as preparing food is one thing, but eating the food is quite another. The apostle Paul shows us how to accept the Lord's death. Romans 6 discloses to us that every one of us has died. Romans 7, though, tells us why I as a Christian, having died, am still not dead. Why am I who died yet alive today? Romans 6 is the objective truth, whereas Romans 7 is the subjective experience. Romans 6 is fact, while Romans 7 is experience. Many Christians today know Romans 6 quite well. They understand they are no longer in bondage to sin, they have been discharged from the law, and they must reckon themselves as dead to sin daily. Though they understand, nothing seems to work.

The teaching and I are far apart. The teaching is, "I have been crucified with Christ;" even so, I say I am still alive. The teaching says I am no longer in bondage to sin; even so, I say sin is still with me. The teaching says I have been freed from the bondage of the law; even so, I say I am yet under law. What really is the explanation? We shall find it in Romans 7.

Romans 7 unveils a hidden flaw in us; which is to say, that we do not approve of what God has done and we do not accept His verdict. Why did God crucify us? When He crucified us with His Son, He was telling us we were absolutely useless and hopeless: that we were beyond repair or improvement: that apart from our being crucified, there is really neither any use nor hope. Therefore, the cross stands as an *evaluation* of us. The evaluation of the cross is that you and I are worthy of death. This is God's appraisal of you and me. If we truly accept the cross as our evaluation, then we know for certain we are totally useless and without any good. We too will say with God that we are worthy of death. God has already declared that except we die, you and I are utterly without hope. If we truly acknowledge this, can we possibly still think of doing any good works?

Recently the Chinese government proclaimed a new law against opium smoking. All who smoke opium after being reformed will be shot. Suppose the government catches a person who has smoked it after being reformed. What do you think that person will do? Will he ask a doctor to give him some injections so that he may quit smoking it before he dies? It would be meaningless if he should do so. Why? Because he is already a condemned prisoner. He will not think of doing the slightest good or of reforming. He will just wait for his death. Similarly speaking, God has said we are worthy to die; that we are beyond repair and reform. If, then, his verdict for us is death, why should we think of doing any good work to try to improve ourselves?

In spite of our admission that it was useless for us to repair or improve ourselves *before* we were saved, we nonetheless attempt to do these very same kinds of things *after* we were saved so that we might please God. How we resolved many times to be good! How we made many spiritual promises to God! We have told Him we would do whatever He wanted us to do. We promised Him we would rise up early in the morning. We promised to be zealous the next day. Many have been our promises, yet how many have we actually fulfilled? One sister from the Western world told me that she had promised God concerning thirty different items in her life, but she was not able to fulfill even one. This only demonstrates the fact that we have not accepted God's evaluation of us, nor have we acknowledged His verdict about us. We have been destined to die, yet we have been busy thinking of getting a physician or changing to better dress or whatever.

Oh, let us realize that the cross expresses God's despair of men! It announces His hopelessness towards men! It is God's way of saying that He can neither repair nor improve us, He can only crucify us. What is surprising is, that though we have already known this fact of our utter corruption and, therefore, our crucifixion, we nevertheless continue to claim we are not so bad. Accordingly, we made resolutions today and will make even more resolutions tomorrow: O God, I will not lose my temper hereafter: O God, perhaps my last resolution was not firm enough: this time, O God, I will make it firmer. Thus do we make resolution after resolution. Such was the way, in fact, that Paul followed: "to will is present with me, but to do that which is good is not" (Rom. 7.18b). Always resolve, yet always fail. Like Paul before us, for many of us today this is our common experience too. Have we not resolved and promised long enough? Let us heed once and for all what God says about us: He says we are worthy of death because we are useless and hopeless.

"I have been crucified with Christ" means that God was disappointed in me and also that I, like Paul, have despaired of myself too. God had seen me through and through. He knew that I had neither usefulness nor hope. So I too have reckoned myself as hopeless and confessed that I could never please God. There is nothing God can do but to put me to death. All who are in the flesh have absolutely no hope and are therefore worthy of death.

Recently I have been to see a number of families. In some, the husbands have been sick; in others, the wives have been sick; and in still others, the children have been sick. When these families begin to give up hope, they say to me, "If it be God's will let this one or that one be taken earlier." Why do they say this? Because there is no more hope. Being hopeless, it is better to die early. Has not God said to us that we were hopeless, and that therefore He could do nothing but have us crucified? Can we not also say to ourselves that since we are hopeless, it is better for us to be crucified?

Here is our problem: on the one hand, we are most familiar with the evaluation of Romans 6; on the other hand, we make the resolutions of Romans 7: we are still promising God, we still consider ourselves as possessing some good. However plain Romans 6 speaks, what we nonetheless do is Romans 7. Romans 6 is God's verdict of Paul that he was of no use. Romans 7 is Paul's reluctant admission that he was indeed of no use. God has seen us through and through. And having seen us clearly, He has already given up hope about us. He deems us to be worth nothing and declares that we are utterly useless. So what do we say in response? Were we also to say we are disappointed and consider ourselves useless, we would immediately be delivered. The reason God has allowed you and me to continue on and on to be proud and jealous and ill-tempered and dishonest is to let these and other sins so frustrate us that IIe will finally be able to show us that we are truly undone. Yet we make resolution after resolution, hoping all the time we may do better, though we end up no better than before. Such is the experience of Paul in Romans 7. Because Romans 6 is but a teaching, it requires the experience of Romans 7 to convince us of our total inability and make us realize it is a fact.

If anyone will confess he is utterly corrupt, I will say Hallelujah, amen, in response. I, Watchman Nee, am corrupt to the core. Hallelujah! Paul in his day was reduced to hopelessness. He had suffered many years. He was fit to be crucified. Today if you acknowledge you are useless, then you will quickly be delivered. It is quite true that all sinners who try to do good will never be saved. Yet likewise, all saints who resolve to do good will never experience victory either. Let us readily accept the fact that the cross of Christ has not evaluated us incorrectly. Let us gladly accept the Bible's verdict of us: I was useless yesterday, I am useless today, and will be useless tomorrow; I am forever useless.

Why does God wish us to accept the evaluation of the cross? He knows that by accepting its evaluation, we shall be willing at last to accept the Lord to be our holiness, perfection and victory. But if we harbor a little hope in our breast, God will have to bring us to no hope so as to enable us to accept the cross. God must bring us to this place by means of the Romans 7 experience so as to make us realize our disability once and for all and acknowledge it.

Strangely enough, however, even though many have at last seen their inability, they still do not experience the victory. Why is this so? It is because God has still another aspect in this matter of yielding for us to see.

(2) I Will Not

Yesterday I met a sister who took two hours to tell me her history of decades of defeats. As she talked, I smiled. I asked her whether she had failed enough to give up any hope. True, she confessed her inability, but she lacked one thing. Merely to acknowledge our inability will not give us victory. Acknowledging an inability is one thing, giving it up altogether is another. I told this sister it was good of her to acknowledge her inability, but did she realize that she was still trying to be able to overcome? If she knew she was not able, she should cease from her own works. She admitted she could do nothing, yet she was still hoping she could do something. So I reiterated the following to her a number of times: "Do you not see you are still working? Do you not understand that you are still attempting to overcome?" She had struggled and strived, and hence she could not overcome. Once again I urged this sister to accept the cross, to acknowledge her inability, and to cease from trying and expecting victory. She asked me what she must therefore do. I answered by saying that if she felt she needed to do something, then she would invariably fail. But her conclusion to the matter was this: "Yes, I admit that when I work, I fail; yet if I do not work, will I not fail even more?" Truly, the problem with many people is just here: knowing clearly they have neither strength nor usefulness, they still insist on struggling hard; and consequently, they have no victory.

Hence victory in the area of yielding has these two essential aspects: first, to acknowledge that God's evaluation of you is correct; and second, to cease even thinking of victory, because you have given up all hope. One brother said to me, "But I cannot believe." "Then tell God that you cannot believe," I said, "for He simply wants you to confess your unbelief."

To say with conviction that " I have been crucified with Christ" means that hereafter I do not care about victory or defeat because I lay everything in the hands of Christ. It means to let go of my hold on the matter of overcoming and to cease caring anymore. I will tell God that henceforth I commit myself to Him, and that victory is His business and not mine. One brother asked me how he could enter into victory. My response was to "let go." "Let go" means that "this is not my business to perform."

We may indeed have the heart attitude towards God that confesses, "I cannot but explode with anger. I cannot suppress my temper forever, nor can I yield. But from now on, I relinquish my control, I let go of myself completely." Yet unfortunately, although we come to God and say we cannot and we will not, we nevertheless take ourselves back when we leave His presence. Oh, let us learn that what we bring to God of ourselves when we come to Him we must leave with Him when we go. He who knows how to cast off to God and leave it there will be delivered.

Once I brought a manuscript to a sister to be copied. I made a special trip to her for that purpose. But when I left I unconsciously brought it back with me. It was obvious she could not copy that manuscript even though she wanted to. This is the way we often pray today. With our mouth we say, O God, please help me. After prayer, however, we bring ourselves back home.

It is exceedingly important for us to let go. Let us pray, "O God, I cannot overcome, neither do I will to overcome, nor will I try to overcome." Such is the meaning of the Biblical statement, "I have been crucified with Christ." How excellent is that statement!

In the early morning Satan may accuse you of being nothing better, for you remain the same. Do you begin to worry? Do you attempt to do something about it? If only you will declare, "I knew long ago I am utterly corrupt, and I have given up hope: I will not try to improve myself," then you will immediately rise above the despondency. How marvelous this is, because it is a matter not of change, but of exchange. Simply lay hold of God's accomplished fact. If you had had any good, God would not have crucified you. Yet because you *are* so utterly corrupt, He has crucified you and put Christ in you. So that you must let go of yourself. And how do you put this into practice? You simply need to say, "God, I cannot do good, nor will I try to do good. O Lord, hereafter I am finished. I am absolutely incapable, and *I will not* even try to be able." Dare you let go like this?

An elderly physician of almost seventy years of age had a struggle with his cigar. One day in the meeting he mentioned about his fight to overcome cigar smoking. A young man who knew God well was there. He told the physician, "If I were you, I would not fight." "Do you know that with my fighting I still cannot overcome? Yet if I stop fighting it altogether, how much more trouble I will have!" "Not so," replied the young man. "If I were you, I would say to God, O God, I cannot help but smoke. Yet God, You take me off smoking." The physician saw the logic of the counsel. So he prayed out of his heart, declaring, "O God, I have no way to quit smoking. Now I quit trying. O God, I hand it over to you. I will not do anything but ask You to take me off smoking." He usually smoked twelve to twenty cigars a day, and he had smoked for fifty years. But after the day he yielded to the Lord, he told people the next day that so far as he could remember, that was the first morning in his life he had had no desire to smoke.

If you think you can be holy, you will doubtless fail. If you think you can be perfect, you will surely fail. If you think you can be patient, you will certainly fail. This is because God has already considered you beyond repair and reform. Can you say with Paul, "I have been crucified with Christ," I am utterly corrupt, I am wholly useless, and I deserve to be crucified? This is what Paul meant by his Galatian statement. I asked a brother in Peking about this matter of overcoming: "Are you finished trying?" "Thank and praise God, I am finished," replied that brother. This is an essential condition for victory. You must see before God that you are absolutely of no use and that you cannot be repaired or reformed. All you can do is to pray, "Lord, hereafter I commit all to You; from now on You will do everything for me."

Even with *this* conviction, however, some brothers and sisters who have confessed they are unable, even finished, and that they have been crucified with Christ, *still* find themselves defeated. Why do they still not experience victory? It is because they need *one other word* before they can experience victory in overcoming. And this is the second condition for victory.

B. Believing—"that life which I now live in the flesh I live in faith, the faith which is in the Son of God"

Let us recapitulate what has been said up till now. God says

I am utterly corrupt; I too say I am utterly corrupt. God says I am useless; I also say I am useless. God says I deserve nothing but death; I likewise say I deserve only death: "It is no longer I that live, but Christ liveth in me." This is a fact. According to fact, I no longer am living today. It is Christ who lives in me. Why is it no longer I who live? Two minus one is one; subtract Adam from me, and what is left, obviously, is Christ. The two live together, but one has been removed, so Christ is the only One left in us. This is fact. But how do I manifest it? In no other way except by *believing*.

(1) Believe God's Fact

The gospel of God tells us that He has given His Son to us. His Son has become righteousness, holiness and redemption (see 1 Cor. 1.30 mg.). Actually, we do not need to accept Him as our life in order to have Him share His perfection, patience and gentleness with us, because He already is our life. The Scriptures show us that Christ is our head (see Eph. 1.22, 4.15; Col. 1.18). Just as the head of a man feels and cares for and controls the body, so Christ is towards us who are Christians. We do not need to ask Him to be our head that we may be His body. Today He *is* the head, and we *are* members of His body. This is faith. Negatively, we have yielded; yet positively speaking, do we now believe that Christ is our head who is feeling, and caring for and controlling us? God's word states that Christ is the head; do you believe that He is at present caring for you?

The word of God also reveals to us that Christ is the vine and we are the branches (see John 15.5). It is not that He will become our vine and we will become His branches. It is not that in the near future when our spiritual life is more advanced than it is now we will then become His branches and He will become our vine. We should bear fruit as He does. We should be filled with virtues as He is filled with virtues. For He has given his "sap"—that is to say, His life and fruit-producing power—to us.

He is now already the trunk, and we are already His branches. He is presently supplying to us His life with His perfection and holiness and all virtues. Do we believe this? Do we believe that He now *is* our trunk and we *are* His branches?

When you believed Him as your Savior, you were already perfectly joined to Him. Do you believe this? You do not need to figure out how you can be joined to Him since God has already made you and Him into one tree. Can you now believe that He shall be towards you even as the physical trunk of a tree is towards its branches? It is not that you bear fruit *for Him*, but rather that He bears fruit *through you*.

God has also indicated in His word that the union of the Lord Jesus and us is similar to the way food is to us: Christ is the blood we drink and the meat we eat (see John 6.51-58). He is the One who sustains our lives. And just as physical food supplies the needs we have in us, without which supply we would die, just so is the Lord Jesus to us as our spiritual food.

God in His word assures us that we are joined to Christ. Christ is our head, our trunk and our food. We do not need to ask God to give us power so that we can live as Christ lived, because He has given His Son to us to be our power of life, to care and live for us. He has given His Son to us that the perfection, communion, joy and riches of His Son may live out through us. Formerly, in our ignorance we always thought of establishing our own holiness, instead of submitting to God's holiness. Now, though, we have, negatively, ceased from our own works, yet this is not quite enough. God's word says that since He gives His Son to us as life, we must, positively, *believe* in Him as our life. Thus shall He manifest all that He is through us. Whenever and whatever our need is, He will supply it. Let us *believe* that He has already done so.

The genius of victory lies in its having no need to overcome gradually. By faith we know Christ is our victory. For victory *is* Christ, and faith brings forth all that is Christ's in us. The grace of God has already given the Lord Jesus to us; today by faith we accept all that God has given us so that the life, power, liberty and holiness of Christ may be manifested in our body.

This mystery of union is God's work by which the unsearchable riches of Christ become ours. Do we believe this? All that is Christ's is ours. Do we believe that God has given us His holiness, perfection, life, power and riches? God has joined us to Christ causing Him to be our head, our trunk and our food. Do we believe that Christ is now our righteousness and sanctification and redemption? Do we believe He is presently living out His life in us? God has indeed invited us, nay, He has *commanded* us to believe. Our union with Christ is patterned after the union of Christ with God; therefore, His patience, gentleness, purity and goodness are all ours. Just as in initial salvation we previously believed Him to be our righteousness, so today let us likewise believe Him to be our holiness. Yet how many fail in this respect. They know God's way of victory, but they do not have the faith. They know their inability, but they do not know Christ's ability. They see the total corruption of their flesh, but they do not see the riches of Christ as God's gift to them.

How do we receive this gift? By doing nothing; let us simply accept it. As we believe God's word, we receive His gift. This is the gospel. We receive by faith, and the Holy Spirit takes our faith to be the starting point for God's miracle to be done in us. People who have not experienced the mighty power of God may not take this seriously. But to the experienced, it is a precious reality. As we believe that all which is in the Lord is ours, the Holy Spirit will cause it to be truly ours. What a gospel this is! Whatever belongs to Christ becomes ours through faith! By faith this perfect life of Christ will daily live out itself in our body of death. With faith, it is not only "no longer I that live," but also "Christ liveth in me." Truly, beyond any doubt, Christ lives in us. Yet it is all because of faith.

(2) Believe You Received, and You Shall Have

God cannot make us believe what we will not believe. Some

people, when they are asked to let go, do let go. But with others, they may say they believe, yet they will wait and see. It is indeed important to yield, although the most essential thing is believing that the Lord Jesus is now living out His victory in us. Yield, and also believe. By believing what God says about Christ dying on the cross for us, we receive eternal life. Likewise, by believing that the Lord Jesus lives in us, we receive the life that wins.

I know the failure of many lies just here: they cannot believe that the Lord has already taken up His dwelling place in them, and thus they will not believe the Lord overcomes for them. Once I asked a sister if she had let go of herself. She said she had. "How did you let go?" "I told God I am utterly helpless, so I will give up trying," she replied. She then told me her prayer to God: "Hereafter, O God, I commit my all to You, be it victory or defeat." "Do you have victory?" I inquired. "I dare not say I do," she answered. "Why not?" "Because I do not feel I have overcome, nor have I seen any effect." I therefore said to her, "If you believe in God's fact and believe that the Lord Jesus who lives in you is victory, you should right away believe you *have* the victory. But if you look for results, you will never have it."

To receive the grace of victory is the same as to have received at conversion the grace of forgiveness. Do you not tell a sinner that because Jesus has died on the cross for him his sins shall be forgiven as soon as he believes? And if he believes, his sins are remitted. So you ask him if he believes, and he says he does. You then ask him if his sins are forgiven. He says no. Why? Because he has heard people say that if sins are forgiven there will be joy and peace; but he still does not have this joy and peace. He goes on to tell you that he is determined to pray until he obtains joy and peace, and only then will he dare to say that his sins are forgiven. Now if you hear such a response, will you not tell him that even if he prays for a whole year waiting for joy and peace, he will not have these feelings? When will he have both joy and peace? You will doubtless tell him that only when he believes will he have joy and peace. The same is true with respect to victory after forgiveness. As you fulfill the condition for victory by yielding and letting go of yourself, you should at once believe that now you have the life that wins. For the Son of God is waiting to live out His victory in you. *Believe*, and the result shall follow. *Wait* for the result, and you will never have the victory.

In the event you are waiting for the result before you dare to say you have the life that wins, then in reality what you believe is your own experience rather than the word of God. But as soon as you believe in God's word, then the experience, feeling and victory will follow. Paul did not say, "I feel I have overcome." What he declared was that "that life which I now live in the flesh I live in faith, the faith which is in the Son of God." In spite of your feeling cold and unexcited, you may still thank and praise God that "that life which I now live in the flesh I live in faith, the faith which is in the Son of God."

Do not look at me as though to find a most energetic person, for the truth of the matter is that I feel tired every day. Never is there a morning that I get up but what I feel frigid; never a day passes that I feel elated. Satan has come to me many times, accusing me: "You do not feel happy and you are so cold emotionally every day; is this Christ living in you? In days past you were frigid and without feeling; now you are still frigid and without feeling. Is this the victory of Christ?" When this happens, God gives me an answer at once: "If I *feel*, then *I* am living; but if I *believe*, then it is the *Son of God* who is living. I feel with my flesh, but I believe in the Son of God. I feel with physical senses, but I believe in the word of God." God says if you fulfill His conditions of yielding and believing, then Christ will live out His victory in you. Hence you should pray: "O God, I praise and thank You that what I feel is nothing, for in this matter the biggest lie of Satan is feeling; it is a close ally of the enemy himself. O God, I thank You that I can believe Your word instead of my feeling. For only Your word is true, whereas feeling is undependable." When you confront temptation in the form of feeling, boldly declare that you live by the faith of the Son of God.

As you let go and believe, you shall see the son of God fighting on your behalf. He will gain the victory for you. He will take away your bad temper, your hardness, your pride, your jealousy. Praise the Lord that from ancient days to the present hour there is only one Overcomer in the whole universe! Praise Him that all the people in the world are feeble! We are all defeated, we are all useless! The Lord alone is Victor! We cannot help but boast in Christ Jesus! For in truth, what *have* we that has not been received? Of what can we boast? Praise to the Lord, we have not changed, we have only been exchanged!

Let us fulfill these basic conditions: on the one hand, yield— recognizing that you cannot and you will not; on the other hand, believe in the Son of God and live—believe in God's fact of Christ living in you and believe that you have received. This is victory. Hallelujah, all is done by Him! May we ask God to show us that all is done by His Son without our help. This, and only this, can be called victory.

.5 | Yielding

But he [Jesus] said, The things which are impossible with men are possible with God. (Luke 18.27)

He hath said unto me, My grace is sufficient for thee: for my power is made perfect in weakness. Most gladly therefore will I rather glory in my weaknesses, that the power of Christ may rest upon me. (2 Cor. 12.9)

"One thing thou lackest Yet"

In Luke 18.27 the Lord Jesus is recorded as saying: "The things which are impossible with men are possible with God." We all know the context in which the Lord said this word. A young man had come to Him and asked, "What shall I do to inherit eternal life?" (v.18) Since he asked what he should do, the Lord answered, "Thou knowest the commandments, Do not commit adultery, Do not kill, Do not steal, Do not bear false witness, Honor thy father and mother" (v.20). Our Lord mentioned these five commandments to show that there were things to do and things not to do if anyone thought of inheriting eternal life (the uncreated life of God) by works. The young man regarded himself as having observed all these commandments from his youth up. But the Lord reminded him, "One thing thou lackest yet" (v.22a).

There is a principle to be learned from this passage. When the young man asked the Lord what he should do to inherit eter nal life, our Lord told him only five of the commandments. Why not tell him all? Why, after having mentioned but five of them, did the Lord add, "One thing thou lackest yet"? The only reason was to let him know his inability. Eternal life is a gift; it is God's grace; it cannot be earned by man's works. But the young man , did not understand; he even boasted that he had observed all/ five of these commandments from his youth. The Lord knew, however, that there was one thing this young man could *not* do; so He added, "One thing thou lackest yet." And we know the end of the story: the young man failed to inherit by works.

Now concerning this matter of victory, it runs along the same principle. Some of you may claim that you are not as proud or jealous or hard as many other people. In fact, you may be better in many areas of life than are others. Yet God knows there is one area in your life which you cannot overcome. He leaves this thing in you to cause you to see that with man this is impossible. You deduce you can do *all* things because you have not committed adultery, murdered, stolen, or borne false witness and have honored your parents. Were anyone to ask you if you have overcome, you would probably answer that you have overcome in this thing and that thing. And you would thus reckon that *all* is well. However, the question today is not how many things you *have* overcome, but is there one particular thing you cannot overcome? God allows this thing to remain in your life so as to convince you of your inability.

We have already seen that God's verdict for us is that we deserve to be crucified. For He knows us through and through. He knows we cannot overcome sin, nor can we even do good. He has seen us through clearly but we see ourselves dimly. So that when God declares we are worthless and useless, we still consider ourselves to be somewhat good and useful. Notwithstanding our claim to be good, however, God declares to each of us: "One thing thou lackest yet." Some people are troubled by their hot temper; others, by their hardness. One may not be proud or jealous, but his hardness always follows him: "One thing

thou lackest yet." There must be one area which he has not overcome, one sin that he has no power to conquer. Someone may
not be proud or jealous or hard or hot-tempered, but his mouth
operates incessantly. He cannot live without talking. He may pro-
claim that he has committed neither this nor that nor the other
sin, but the Lord will say to him, "One thing thou lackest yet."
Or someone else is tight with money. Throughout his life he has
not committed any gross sin; nonetheless, he commits the sin
of greediness. The love of money is the basic ingredient of his
conduct. Hence God says to him: "One thing thou lackest yet."
And this one thing proves his inability. People long to have a
perfect life manifested in them, but they have one thing which
testifies against them. Thus the first condition is to confess this
one thing. With some, it is pride; with others, it is jealousy; with
some, it is talkativeness; with others, it is unclean thoughts. And
with many, it is even *more* than one thing.

What was the Lord trying to say? Salvation is impossible with
men; life eternal is impossible with men; victory is impossible
with men; abundant life is impossible with men. Yet the young
man refused to believe he was unable. How bold, strong and confident were the phrases that passed from his lips: "from my youth
up," "all these things," "I have observed." What a majestic-sounding
answer! How elated he must have felt! He thought he had all
in his life under control. But the Lord responded with: "One thing
thou lackest yet." You may argue that you do not have the sins
of pride, jealousy, hardness, impure thoughts, or talkativeness
that I have mentioned. But let me echo our Lord Jesus: "One
thing thou lackest yet." Go home and ponder what thing it is that
you lack.

God Wants Men to See Their Inability

May I speak frankly to you that God's verdict is, you are
unable. He concludes you are not able because He knows you
through and through. He has already said so: and what will you

say? Do you know why God allows you even up to this present time to fail again and again since you were saved?

Many brothers and sisters weep over a particular sin they cannot overcome. And perhaps you do so too. But I thank and praise God for such inability! Yet please do not feel by my saying this that I am being unsympathetic towards you in your sorrow over this one sin that seems to entangle you relentlessly. God wants you to see that you are not able. He does not need to show you many of your sins; He merely allows one thing to stay in your life to demonstrate to you your inability. Have you realized your inability?

One sister was able to overcome all sins except the one of lying. As she spoke, she lied. She knew this was the one sin she could not overcome. Another sister easily lost her temper. She could not control herself. The least provocation would ignite her hot temper. As she exploded, she confessed. This was most embarrassing to her. Yet she was totally helpless. A brother was able to overcome many sins except that of smoking. He was a good brother, but he had no way to quit this habit. Another sister had victory over a number of other sins, except the one of continual snacking.

Why do so many Christians have so many different experiences of this kind? It is God's way of convincing and convicting them of their inability. He has seen so thoroughly your inability, but you continue to maintain that you are able. God says you are hopeless, but you say you have hope. Do you understand that your many heartbreaking failures and shameful defeats are God's way of demonstrating to you your inability? Have you failed enough? Has God finally convinced you you can never prevail? He allows you to fail once, twice, ten times, even twenty or a hundred times. Have there been sufficient proofs of your inability? He wants you to see your inability so that you may at last confess, "O God, I am not able." For a person to be saved, he needs first to confess that he is not able to save himself. Likewise, for one to overcome, he must also first acknowledge his inability.

And as soon as one comes to *this* point, God will immediately commence working. Unfortunately, the young man who came to the Lord Jesus went away sorrowful. How sad that though he knew his inability, he left in despair!

God gave the law to men for two thousand years. What was the purpose of God's giving the Ten Commandments to the children of Israel? He gave them these not for them to *keep* but for them to *break*. How is this so? Because God knew men could not keep these commandments; He knew they were all sinners. But men would not accept God's verdict until they had failed in their own eyes; only then would they confess that they were sinners. The book of Romans tells us that God gave the law not for men to keep but for them to violate. After they failed to keep the law, they had to accept God's verdict and capitulate. God used two thousand years of human history to cause men to know their inability before He could give Christ to men for them to accept Him and be saved.

For the past two thousand years, many sinners have been saved. We who name the name of Christ are saved sinners; we should therefore be fully yielded. Nevertheless, we try to reform our ill-temper, pride or whatever. We may make some progress, yet these things are merely suppressed. Formerly our bad temper showed itself outwardly; but now it is suppressed within. Previously, our pride was seen externally; now it is pressed inwardly. But though they be suppressed, they have *not* been overcome. Thus will God convince us finally of our inability. He declares that no one can overcome his sin; no one is able to deal with it.

Now when you realize you are helpless, you come to God for deliverance. The first step to take is to tell Him, "O God, I cannot, and I will not. I am finished, I give up trying, I will fight no more." This is yielding. This marks the first step towards deliverance. Formerly I thought I could change my pride somewhat; now, Lord, I will not try again. Formerly, I reasoned I could improve my temper a little; now, Lord, I quit altogether. Formerly, I imagined I could somehow control my tongue; now,

Lord, I give up. I cannot, I will not try to change, I give up completely.

Yielding Is Letting Go

When you see that the Lord was crucified for you, what happens as you believe? Is it not that you cease from improving yourself since you now see that you are saved by faith? In a similar way, when you see that the Lord took you with Him to the cross, you have no need to fight for self-improvement or to reform. Instead, believe that the Lord lives in you and overcomes for you. You should immediately cease your own works and let God deliver you. Tell Him, "O God, I can never be good. Henceforth I will not try to do good. I give up; I let go. From now on, it is no longer my problem." This is yielding; this is letting go.

Some people find it most difficult to let go. Whenever temptation comes, there is always a battle. Whenever temper arises, there is usually a fight. If the resolution on the first occasion fails, a stronger resolution will be made the next time. The more resolves, the more defeats. The more promises, the more failures. No matter how strong the next resolution is, the situation is as Romans 7 describes it: "To will is present with me, but to do that which is good is not. For the good which I would I do not: but the evil which I would not, that I practise" (v.18b–19). No promise is right because your hand has not let go. You yourself are still taking care of your affairs; therefore you cannot say with conviction, "I have been crucified with Christ"; neither can you say, "It is no longer I that live, but Christ liveth in me." Death means letting go, putting hands off, no more care, and no longer control. Only when it becomes impossible to you does it begin to be possible with God. So that the first important step is for you to take your hands off.

A certain brother in Tientsin asked me how to let go, for he had tried to do so but could not. "Brother," I inquired, "what is your position at the company?" "I am head of the cloth department," he replied. "Suppose your general manager were to tell you today that the company will lay you off next month. What would you do?" I asked. "Well, by the next month I would have to quit," he said. "Suppose in the next month the new head arrives and you hand all things in the department over to him. But after you have made the transfer, suddenly an agent comes to you and reports that a certain cloth is going to increase in price after two days. What would you do then?" "If this report had come earlier, I would have begun to figure how much of this kind of cloth we have in stock and how much we should buy to increase the inventory. But by this time I have already handed the department's affairs over to the new head. So I am glad I have nothing to do but to watch." This is an excellent example of taking hands off. This is yielding to the fact that "I have been crucified with Christ." Tell the Lord, "Lord, I resign not because I am able but because I am helpless. My temper, pride, hardness and jealousy remain with me, but there is nothing I can do. I can only hand over myself. Henceforth everything is in Your hand." Do not be stirred by God's opposing agents. There are legions of the enemy's agents; daily they will tempt you to do something. But you have committed yourself into the hands of the Lord. All is well if you neither care nor work. This is called victory. This is yielding.

Satan Tempts You to Bestir Yourself

Do you know what the basic temptation is? One brother says he is often tempted to lose his temper. Another brother says he is frequently tempted to be harsh. Still another brother says he is usually tempted into unclean thoughts. Yet another brother says he is tempted to be talkative all the time. A thousand persons seem to have a thousand different temptations. Yet there is but one temptation in the whole world. Notwithstanding all the various temptations to bad temper, pride, greediness, adultery and so forth, the enemy really has but one temptation, and that is, to bestir the saints. Satan does not tempt you so that you lose your temper, become proud or greedy or adulterous. He simply tempts you to bestir yourself. If only he succeeds in bestirring you to *do* something, he gains the victory. Oh that I had enough tears to cry out, "Don't be stirred!" Because once you have been stirred up to take action, you have failed. Whether you struggle with Satan, fight with him or resist him, so long as you are bestirred, he obtains the victory. Do keep in mind that our victory lies in being spectators; our victory is achieved in detachment. How wonderful if we could see it—that God sets us aside and lets His Son overcome for us!

"The flesh lusteth against the Spirit, and the Spirit against the flesh; for these are contrary the one to the other; that ye may not do the things that ye would" (Gal. 5.17). It does not say here that *we* strive against the flesh, nor that the flesh strives against *us*. It says instead that the Spirit lusts against the flesh and the flesh lusts against the Spirit. *We* are not involved; only the Spirit and the flesh are opposed to each other. What is it that we like to do? We like to sin, we like uncleanness. Yet we are to be the helpless observers, since the Spirit and the flesh are the ones that strive against each other. No place is given for us to participate. And yet such is God's deliverance. We sit on the sidelines to watch the striving of the Holy Spirit against the flesh and vice versa. Such is the way of deliverance.

When I was first saved, I heard a story about a little girl who in her testimony revealed the extent to which she truly understood this matter of victory. During the Keswick Convention, someone asked the little girl, "How do you overcome when you are tempted?" "Formerly, whenever the devil came knocking at my door," she reported, "I would immediately say, 'Don't you come in, don't you come in!' But this always ended up in defeat. Now, though, whenever the devil knocks at the door, I at once say to the Lord: 'Lord, You open the door.' The Lord goes forward to do so. And as soon as the devil sees the Lord, the devil says:

'I am sorry, I have knocked at the wrong door.' And with that he turns and flees."

In the course of our being tempted, if we cry out, "O Lord, here comes temptation; O Lord, save me, save me," the devil will come in before the door is even opened. Today, leave it to the Lord to deal with the devil. The longer, the more anxious and more repetitious the prayer, the firmer is the holding on of our hands. One brother reminded us that when Peter was sinking, he merely cried out, "Lord, save me." Just ask simply in one sentence, and this will indicate you are taking your hands off. If you continue to cry out, saying "O Lord, save me," repeating it many times, you are already defeated. I call such prayer "hanging-on prayer." The more you pray such prayer, the more it proves you have not let go, but are hanging on to the situation. You try to use prayer to attain victory; you are still thinking of using your own strength to gain the triumph. As a consequence you will not have victory. Stop crying, and you will come into victory. Do remember that Satan wants you to be stirred up, *even if you are bestirred to pray.*

Previously, you would burn when you heard any pricking words. What would you do today if someone were to pick on you incessantly? If you were to say to the Lord, "O Lord, this is not my business; victory is Your business; I confess I cannot control my temper; but Lord, You are responsible," this would be called letting go. And the Lord would live out His patience through you. You could praise and thank God and say, "Lord, I could not care less." But suppose you felt you could no longer bear the provocation, and you pray, "O Lord, save me, for I am quickly losing my control." Fifteen minutes would pass like fifteen hours. Now although you would not explode outwardly, you would nonetheless be burning already within. And this would show you have not overcome. Satan does not seek for an explosion of your temper; he merely wants you to be agitated. And thus will he win.

Victory is when you are not stirred up to do. Victory means you pay no attention; it means you could not care less. Your calmness, aloofness and carelessness are rightfully called a letting go. Victory does not depend upon you, since you have already died. Instead, it is Christ who gains the victory for you. You have died and Christ lives—and this is called victory.

At the conference in Chefoo, many brothers and sisters crossed the threshold to victory. One sister had a tragic past. Her husband as well as her mother-in-law ill-treated her. She patiently endured but had no victory. As I spoke on the life that wins, she accepted the truth. But two days later she came to see me about the way of letting go and letting God. She did not understand how. So I asked the Lord to give me a helpful illustration.

"Have you ever visited a friend by taxi?" I asked. "Yes, I have," she said. "When the car arrives at your friend's door, and just as you are taking money out of your pocket, your friend hurries out the door to pay it for you. You want to pay, but your friend wants to pay for you. You return the money to her, but she gives it right back to you. Has there ever been such a scene in your own experience?" "Yes, indeed." "Now, supposing after she paid the twenty cents fare for you, the driver takes it and leaves and you have your visit with your friend. But because you had still not wanted her to spend her money for you, you suddenly thrust twenty cents into your friend's hand as you are leaving. As she sees you out at the end of the visit, however, she quickly thrusts the money back into your hand. But then, you both pass the money back and forth between yourselves until finally you leave the money on the street and say to your friend that you are leaving. Even so, you wonder if your friend will pick up the money. What if she does not, and a passerby should take it? What if a driver should pick it up? or a little child would see it and take it? You therefore stealthily look back to see if your friend has retrieved it. To your chagrin she has not picked it up. As you walk on, you cast another look behind you. Let me tell you, if you periodically continue to look back, your friend will never pick up the money for sure. But if you were to leave the money on the street and say to your friend that the money was there for her to pick up, and then you walked away without caring in the slightest who would get it, without a doubt your friend would pick it up." As I finished saying this, she understood; and accordingly, she entered into the life that wins.

The above example is unfortunately how many commit themselves to God. On the one hand, they say they cannot; on the other hand, they worry and look. If you care, God will let you take care and will not take over. But if you do not care, God will care for you and take the whole responsibility on himself. Yielding and letting go is a putting the money on the street and going away without looking back: you could not care less whether a little child, the taxi driver, or a passerby should take it. You simply tell God you have committed all to Him, so that hereafter whether you are bad or good is not your business anymore. In so committing yourself, God will certainly take over. All is well if you simply give up to Him.

If you let go, God will take over. But if you wait for Him to take charge before you let go, God will wait for you to let go before He takes charge. Suppose the brother in the cloth department mentioned above was to be laid off the next month, but that he was also required to *teach* the new head instead of simply handing over the business to him. In that case he would be half responsible during the transfer period. With God, though, this is not possible. Either He accepts all or He accepts nothing. He never works halfway.

We all seem to have a serious sin which is one of unbelief. We take charge over ourselves daily. We think we will fail terribly if we do not take charge and suppress ourselves. But when we preach the gospel to the nations, we tell them that they need not to take care of anything because Christ has already died for them. We tell them that all they need to do is to believe, and they will be saved. In like manner, we have been crucified with Christ, and it is He who now lives in us. Praise and thank God!

Christ is our head, and we are his members. Christ is the vine, and we are the branches. He is our life. He is our all. Let us who are saved therefore move out; let us who have been crucified with Christ care for nothing and let Him begin to bear all our responsibilities!

There was a story recorded in the book that is entitled, *The Christian's Secret of a Happy Life*. A Christian went down a dry well. He lowered himself into it by grasping alternately with his right and left hands the rope tied to the opening of the well. As he lowered himself, he suddenly found himself at the end of the rope. Not knowing how deep the well was, he thought of climbing back to the opening of the well. But it was too late since he did not have the strength anymore to do so. He held on to the rope with both his hands and cried out for help. But the well was situated in a desert and he was at the bottom of the well. No matter how loudly he cried, nobody came to help. Finally he was so exhausted he could hold on to the rope no longer. So he prayed, "O God, let me fall into eternity." And after praying, he loosed his hands from the rope and fell downward. To his amazement it was a mere drop of three inches! He did not fall into eternity but fell back upon the Rock of Ages. Do let go! For the first condition in obtaining the life that wins is letting go. And upon relinquishing your hold you will prevail.

One sister heard the message on how to obtain the life that wins by yielding and believing. She often went to the mountain to pray. I asked her whether she had crossed the threshold to victory. She replied that today in the mountain she had once again dug a new grave and buried herself there. I asked her several times thereafter and she always gave me the same answer. I knew she had dealt with many difficult sins in her life, yet I noticed how worried she was. I prayed for her but to no avail.

One day I asked God to give me utterance that I might help her. On that same day, I heard her playing a hymn. I asked her again how she now was. Her tears fell down and she said, "I have dealt with many things, but there is a small sin I cannot overcome—snacking." To others this problem might mean nothing, but to her she did not consider it a small sin.

As she confessed her problem to me, I smilingly remarked, "This is most excellent! You could be nothing better." But she complained to me as follows: "You say the conditions for obtaining the life that wins are first yielding and second believing. Well, I can neither yield nor believe." "Then you should not yield and you should not believe," I replied. "But do you not say the conditions for victory are first yielding and second believing? Then what can I do if I can neither yield nor believe?" she retorted. "It is well if you neither yield nor believe," I insisted; "for what is yielding? Yielding is a letting go, and letting go is doing nothing. But you have made letting go *a work*. Believing, too, is a doing nothing; yet you have changed believing into *a work*. You find you cannot yield or believe. Alright, why not cross over the threshold to victory just as you are? You have no need to reform, nor even to try to let go. The conditions for victory are for you to simply yield and believe. But you have taken yielding and believing as a works formula, which is completely useless. Just let go of everything and do nothing indeed. Praise if you can; yet do not even try to praise if you cannot. Come to God and throw yourself into His hands; stagger, if necessary, into the bosom of God. *This* is a letting go!"

Oh, how devious we often are. When God says for us to do nothing, we still want to do this thing or that. Many brothers and sisters claim they do let go, yet they turn their letting go into a work. They are still struggling and wasting their strength in letting go and in not letting go. But letting go simply means that I am finished just as I am. This is victory.

After this sister heard me out, she was in a daze for three days because of the greatness of the light. Then she crossed the threshold to victory. God had brought her through.

Our Weakness Is to Be Boasted Of

"He hath said unto me, My grace is sufficient for thee: for

my power is made perfect in weakness. Most gladly therefore will I rather glory in my weaknesses, that the power of Christ may rest upon me" (2 Cor. 12.9). This passage reflects the fact that we must not only confess we are weak and powerless and hopeless but also rejoice in our weaknesses and powerlessness and hopelessness. Does it say we should weep for our weakness? No, instead of weeping we are to rejoice; yet not only to rejoice but even to glory and to boast! The world sighs over its own weaknesses, but overcomers in Christ glory in their weaknesses because of their faith.

Do you sense weaknesses and failures in your life? These are profitable to you since they can help you to overcome.

I met a physician one day in Chefoo. He had been saved for three or four years. He had served in the military for over a decade and was therefore very straightforward and soldier-like. Moreover, there was no doubt about his salvation. Yet he had one habit, which was smoking cigarettes.

When he was in the vast northeast provinces of China, smoking was not a big problem. But now having come to a small place like Chefoo where there were merely seventy or eighty brethren in the church, he could only hide in his home and smoke. Even at home he dared not smoke openly because his wife was a sister in the Lord. In the hospital where he worked, a few nurses were also sisters in the Lord. On the one hand he wanted to smoke, on the other hand he felt uneasy about doing so. If while he was smoking, he heard voices nearby, immediately he would snuff out the cigarette. On the street, before he would light up to smoke he had to look around to see if any acquaintance was there. To quit smoking was something he could not do, yet to continue smoking was something he felt bad about. He was really in a helpless state.

One day after the church meeting he asked for a personal interview at nine o'clock the following morning. He said he had a most important thing to discuss with me. So the next morning as soon as we met, he related his story to me.

"I have smoked for over ten years, I have tried to quit smoking but I cannot. What shall I do?" The more he talked, the more I lifted my head and smiled. "Mr. Nee," he pleaded, "this is a most serious matter to me." "I know," I replied. "There is nothing I can do," he reiterated. "Nothing you can do?" I said; "well, this nothing of yours is better than anything else!" "What do you mean?" he asked.

In reply, I told him this: "I rejoice in my heart, because in this problem of yours, the Lord alone can solve it. You can do nothing, and neither can I. Your wife cannot do anything; brothers and sisters can do nothing. Having such a good patient as you, the Lord Jesus will have a good chance to look you over." "But I have been helpless for over ten years; today it is even *more* serious to me," the doctor stressed. "Indeed, it is impossible to you," I answered, "but nothing is impossible to the Lord. It can be solved with a simple turning."

"Dr. Shih," I went on, "you are a good physician and I have a healthy body. Consequently, you have no use of me nor have I any need of you. In order for you to be able to show forth your skill on me, you can do so only when I am sick, very sick. The more sick I am, the better your skill can be manifested. By the same token, here is the Lord Jesus who today is well able to deal with the problem which you, Dr. Shih, have not been able to deal with." "How can that be so?" he earnestly inquired.

I then showed him 2 Corinthians 12.9 which declares: "My grace is sufficient for thee: for my power is made perfect in weakness. Most gladly therefore will I rather glory in my weaknesses, that the power of Christ may rest upon me." Then I said to him, "Nothing can be better than that you cannot refrain from smoking. If you have thought how good it would be were you able to quit smoking, then you do not yet understand the words of Scripture. For it plainly says here that the power of *Christ* is made perfect in *our* human weakness. According to your view, it would be good not to smoke; but according to God's view, it is better if you cannot help but smoke."

He was dumbfounded by what I had just said, so I continued to explain: "Do not mourn over your smoking, nor consider your inability to quit smoking as bad. Instead, you should pray: 'O God, I thank and praise You, because I smoke. I praise and thank You, for I cannot keep from smoking. Yet I also praise and thank You, because You can make me quit smoking, You can take it away from me.' " "Is it really true that God is able to do this?" he responded. "Truly, God *is* able," I answered. So we prayed together. After I prayed a few words, he also prayed. He really had faith. When he prayed, he spoke like a soldier, straightforwardly saying, "O God, I thank and praise You because I smoke and I cannot stop. O God, I thank and praise You for You are able to make me quit smoking."

After he finished praying, and before his tears were dried, he took up his hat to leave. I asked him, "Dr. Shih, will you smoke again?" He answered, "I, Dr. Shih, am unable to quit smoking, but God is able to make me quit." I now knew the problem was resolved.

In the evening, though, I was concerned about him. So I went to the hospital to see how he was. He said everything was fine. The next morning I inquired again and got the same answer. That same afternoon, when I met him, he said to me, "I spoke with my wife today that what she could not do to make me quit smoking by her quarreling with me over the years, God had cleared up in half an hour. I did not smoke yesterday, and I have not smoked today." Before I left, I questioned him whether he could quit smoking. His answer was that *he* could not, but that the Lord had done it for him. Thus I felt perfectly secure for him.

Do not fancy that you are able to change yourself to be a little better. Even after fifty years you will still be the same. Victory is Christ living in and for you. You may therefore say, Thank God, I cannot, but *Christ* can. I would like to tell the whole world: do not be afraid of men's worst temper or greatest pride; only be fearful lest men do not see Christ's *ability* as well as their own *inability*.

It is good for you to thank God for your victory. But you should also thank Him for your weakness. For the power of Christ is made perfect in your weakness. I thank God that Watchman Nee is most corrupt. I thank Him that once again Christ manifests His power in me. I confess to Him, "O God, I have neither goodness nor righteousness, neither holiness nor patience. But I thank and praise You because I have not, and I will not. Hereafter, O God, I commit my all to You. From now on, it is Your Son who overcomes for me." In this manner, you will instantly obtain victory.

Impossible with Man but Possible with God

In Luke 18, we saw the impossibility of something being done in a young man. In Luke 19, however, we see that in Zacchaeus it *was* made possible: "Behold, Lord, the half of my goods I give to the poor; and if I have wrongfully exacted aught of any man, I restore fourfold" (v.8). He was able to do all this *at once*. What was impossible with the young man was made possible in Zacchaeus. Hence Luke 18 shows us that with men it is impossible; whereas Luke 19 shows us that with God all things are possible. In Luke 18 the *young* man was *un*able but in Luke 19 the *old* man *was* able. In Luke 18 the Lord spoke to the young man who could not hear. In Luke 19 the Lord said nothing, yet the old man believed. It was impossible with the young man because he did not believe that God is able. Salvation came to the house of the old man for he had faith and was therefore a son of Abraham indeed. All was done by God.

Let us thank and praise the Lord. To love, I cannot do; to be patient, I cannot be; to be humble, I cannot be; to be gentle, I cannot be. Yet where does God say in His word that you must do what you can do and must live as you have lived? On the contrary, He commands us to do what we cannot do and live as we have never lived before. Every morning I thank and praise God, because today He will *do* miracles. Every evening I thank and praise God for He has *done* miracles. Today He enables me to endure what I cannot endure; today He causes me to love what I cannot love. Today He makes me do what I cannot do and live in a manner in which I cannot live. Thank and praise Him, daily it is impossible with men, but daily it is possible with God!

6 | Believing

That life which I now live in the flesh I live in faith, the faith which is in the Son of God. (Gal. 2.20b)

Now faith is the assurance of things hoped for, a conviction of things not seen. (Heb. 11.1)

Believe unto Victory

We have seen that the life that wins is none other than Christ himself. It is not my improvement nor my progress. It is not working with my own strength to be like Christ. Victory is Christ living in me and overcoming for me. As He died on the cross for me that I might be saved, so today He lives in me that I may overcome. We have also seen the conditions for victory: one, yielding; and two, believing. We believe that the Son of God lives in us, and we also believe that He lives out his victory through us. In our last discussion we looked more closely than before into the subject of *yielding*. We shall now look more closely than before at this matter of *believing*. Many people have yielded, yet they have no victory. This is because they do not believe. Yielding without believing will not bring in victory, since yielding is the negative side, while believing is the positive side. Only when both of these sides are implemented can victory be assured. And this positive side is what we now wish to look into more thoroughly.

One brother in Chefoo went home after a church meeting

and declared that though he had yielded, he experienced no victory. He remained the same the next day. In fact, he even lost his temper in the store on that very day. So I told him that yielding alone would not guarantee victory, since that was but the negative. What was essential for him to do was to believe with a singleness of heart following his yielding. He accepted the truth and obtained the victory. At the last assembly meeting he stood up and praised God, declaring that this was the first time he had ever praised God for having nothing to boast of and was also the first time he had ever praised God for His having done everything.

What was the experience of the apostle Paul? How did he enter into victory? The first step he took was to yield: "I have been crucified with Christ," he testified. He had already had the experience of "no longer I that live." He then continued by declaring: "That life which I now live in the flesh I live in faith, the faith which is in the Son of God." What he meant here was: I believe the Son of God lives in me; I believe He loved me and gave himself for me.

Let us now inquire as to what faith is, especially the relationship between faith and victory.

Believe in God's Fact

All the things in the Bible are done by God for us. At a conference held in January of 1934, we mentioned that God has given us three things: (1) the covenant He gave us, (2) the fact He accomplished for us, and (3) the promise He bestowed on us. All the things which God did for us were included in these three gifts of covenant, accomplished fact, and promise. When earlier we gave the messages on "the Better Covenant," we talked at great length about this first gift of covenant.* Accordingly, we will not

---

*This series of messages was delivered by the author at a conference held in Shanghai, China, in 1931. For the text of those messages, see Watchman Nee, *The Better Covenant* (New York: Christian Fellowship Publishers, 1982), translated from the Chinese. When consulting this published work, the reader

treat of that subject here. As to God's promise and God's fact, however, we would like to discuss these in some detail. *Promise* is that which God will do for us *in the future*, whereas *fact* is that which God has *already* accomplished in us.

Many people do not know what God's fact is. The Lord Jesus died on the cross for all the world—this is God's fact. But how many have been saved? Only those who have believed. Hence a problem arises, which is to say, that since Christ died for the whole world—and this is God's fact unaffected by men's attitude—why is the whole world not saved? It is because not all in the world receive God's fact *by faith*. Similarly, however, many Christians fail to accept by faith God's fact that Christ lives in them. Christ is the head, and all believers are the body. Just as the head in the physical body feels, manages, controls and responds, so shall it be for the Christian if he allows his spiritual head, even Christ, to feel, manage, control and respond for him. In the face of God's fact, how many Christians really see the Lord Jesus as their head? Today does Christ feel or do they feel? Does Christ manage or do they manage? Does Christ control or do they control? Does Christ respond or do they respond? Where lies the difficulty? In nothing else but a lack of faith.

Perhaps some brothers and sisters will reply that they do believe in Christ as head, yet they cannot believe that the head is responsible for everything. They just cannot believe; they do not understand what faith truly is. The Scripture says that the Lord is the vine and we are the branches. It does not say He will *be* our vine and we will *be* His branches. Whether we believe or not, He nonetheless *is* the vine and we nonetheless *are* the branches. Yet only to those who believe will the spiritual sap flow through them; with the result that they bear fruit. But for those who do not believe, the life of the Lord *cannot* flow through them; therefore, they must themselves labor for any fruit.

---

should be aware that the notation in it indicating the conference was held in 1932 is incorrect. Future reprints of this work will reflect a correction in this dating.—*Translator*

Faith Substantiates God's Fact

Hebrews 11.1 speaks of the significance of faith. It is the only verse in the entire Bible which gives us a definition of faith: "Now faith is the assurance of things hoped for, a conviction of things not seen." In other Bible versions there are a number of other renderings that have been given for the word translated here as "assurance," since this is a most difficult word to translate from the original Greek into English. To be probably the most accurate, this word should be translated as "the giving of substance to"* or "substantiation," which thus means that faith is the ability to substantiate a thing as factual. For example, in this hall where we are meeting, we have before us the shape of the lamp, the color of the wall, and the sound of the organ. How do we substantiate the shape and color and sound to make them real to us? That which can substantiate the existence of color is none other than our two eyes. Suppose there were a picture here also with beautiful colors such as green and red and yellow. These beautiful colors would need the eyes to make them real. If there were no eye, then however beautiful these colors are, nothing could make them real in our own personal experience. By the same token, though the sound of the organ is pleasant, it takes ears to show forth its reality. To one who is deaf, there is no way to substantiate the realness of the music. Neither the eyes nor the touch of the hand can substantiate the sound; only the ears can substantiate the sound and make it enjoyable. Then, too, the shape of a thing may be square, round, plane, triangular or curved; its fact is only to be known either by the touch of the hand or by the sight of the eye. So that the existence of a thing is one matter while the substantiating of it is quite another. There are numerous things in the physical world, but every one of them needs some ability to prove its reality. In the spiritual realm, this ability is what faith is.

---

*Which is the *marginal* rendering of the ASV (1901), the Bible version used throughout this present volume.—*Translator*

Here is a painting with a beautiful scenery of hill, water, flowers and trees. With your eyes you can make real the beauty as well as the existence of that painting. Suppose a man is born blind and he has never seen any color. You try to tell him of the red in the painting, and he will ask what is red color? You say there is green color also, but he says what is green? All you can say to him is that what is red is red color and what is green is green color. Though the painting exists, the blind man cannot enjoy its beauty.

Here is a sister who plays the piano well. Whoever has ears and knows music can appreciate what this sister plays. But he who is deaf and is a stranger to music will not be able to prove the sweetness of the music. Now our faith is just like that. All the facts of God are real and true, but faith alone can verify them. For "faith is the substantiating of things hoped for, the conviction of things not seen" (Heb. 11.1 Darby).

The blind person cannot see the beautiful scenery in a painting. Nevertheless, his inability to see can in no way disprove the existence of the painting. For its existence is a fact, whether a person sees it or not. Its beautiful colors remain unchanged. The question is, can the person be benefited by the painting? He who has eyes is pleased with the painting and is benefited by it. It is the same in the spiritual realm. That the Lord shed His blood and died on the cross for mankind is a fact. Nevertheless, only those who have faith are able to prove this fact and be benefited by it. To those who do not believe, the death of the Lord on the cross may indeed by factual, yet they will not be able to experience it and benefit by it.

Have you now seen the significance of faith? We need faith to prove a spiritual matter just as we need eyes, ears and hands to prove physical matters. In all spiritual affairs, it takes the element of faith to substantiate them. For instance, the Lord is head and we are the members of His body. This union is a fact which cannot be torn asunder. So is the fact of the Lord being the vine and we being the branches. By believing it, we will be benefited by it. Some may say the Lord *is* the vine and they *are* the branches, but they have no experience of spiritual sap nor life nor fruit-bearing. This is because they do not have faith.

What is faith? Faith is not mental apprehension. It is seeing the fact and proving it. You have heard that Christ died on the cross and shed His blood for the remission of sins; and so you say that Christ died on the cross and shed his blood for the remission of sins. You have heard that the Lord is the vine and we are the branches; therefore, you too say that the Lord is the vine and we are the branches. You have heard that the Lord Jesus is your life and He lives in you; whereupon, you too say that the Lord Jesus is your life and lives in you. Nevertheless, you are not able to prove these facts and make them real in experience because you lack faith. In just the same way, you may have let go of yourself because you realize your inability and uselessness. Yet this is but the negative side of victory. You need, positively, to prove Christ by an act of faith — by believing. Is it not most wonderful that in one minute, nay, in one *second*, all the facts which Christ has accomplished can by proven and demonstrated in your life? Such is the substantiating by faith.

How do you know a painting is beautiful? Because you have seen it with your physical eyes. How do you know the riches of Christ? Because you have seen with your spiritual eyes. In the letter to the Colossians, God declares that "in him [Christ] ye are made full" (2.9). But how do you know you are made full in Christ? Because you have seen it with the eye of faith. As you look at yourself, you know you are not complete at all. Even so, are you nonetheless able to declare you are complete in Christ? With the eye of *faith* you *can*. The Lord has given you His riches, grace upon grace. Do you have them? It is not whether you have them in your mind, but whether you *believe* them in your heart.

"Blessed be the God and Father of our Lord Jesus Christ, who hath blessed us with every spiritual blessing in the heavenly places in Christ" (Eph. 1.3). We indeed profess to believe that God has blessed us with every spiritual blessing in the heavenly places in Christ Jesus; nonetheless, where are these blessings? The entire question revolves around the matter of faith, believing that the word of God is true.

The great failure of a Christian is unbelief. Believe, and the fact is proven. See with faith and the fact is substantiated in experience.

There was in England a man of God by the name of H. W. Webb-Peploe. Listen to what he testified:

> Four days afterward, my little child that was with us at the seashore was taken sick and died. I had to carry the little coffin in my arms all the way home, where I buried my little one with my own hands. I returned from the burial and said to myself, "Now you have lost your holiday, have come home in trouble, and you must speak to your people instead of letting your curate speak; you would better tell them about God and his love." I looked to see what lesson was assigned for the Sunday, and found it was the twelfth chapter of Second Corinthians. I read the ninth verse, "My grace is sufficient for thee," and thought, "There is the verse to speak on." I sat down to prepare my notes, but soon found myself murmuring in my tent against God for all he called upon me to bear. I flung down my pen, threw myself on my knees, and said to God, "It is not sufficient, it is not sufficient! Lord, let thy grace be sufficient, O Lord, do!"
>
> The day before I had left home, my mother had given me a beautiful illuminated text, and I had asked the servant to hang it on the wall over my table, that I might find it there when I came back. As I opened my eyes I was saying, "O God, let thy grace be sufficient for me," and there on the wall I saw,
>
> MY GRACE IS SUFFICIENT FOR THEE
>
> The word *is* was in bright green, *My* was in black, and *thee* in black, "MY grace *is* sufficient for THEE." I heard a voice that seemed to say to me, "You fool, how *dare* you ask God to make what is! Get up and take, and you will find it true. When God says '*is*,' it is for you to believe Him, and you will find it true at every moment." That

is turned my life; from that moment I could say, "O God, whatever thou dost say in thy Word I believe, and please God, I will step out upon it."*

This servant of God was so full of joy and thankfulness that he would ask no more of God in this way. The next day he stood in the pulpit and delivered the best message of his life. When people asked him when he had first experienced the enduement of power from heaven, his answer was, after he had returned from burying his little girl. What made the difference was that he had learned to believe.

One brother told me later that after having heard me speak at length, he had gotten nothing out of it. I said to him that this was because he merely listened to me; he should in addition have asked God to speak to him. Accordingly, in the evening he prayed, "O God, cause me to overcome. O God, my temper is very bad, enable me to overcome it." As he prayed, he remembered the prayer of the leper who said to Jesus, "Lord, if thou wilt, thou canst make me clean" (Matt. 8.2b). So he too prayed: "O Lord, if You will, You can make my bad temper leave me." At this point he realized that the Lord was already willing; for in the story, Jesus had said "I will" in response to the leper. Why, then, should he pray this at all? The Lord has accomplished everything and the Lord was willing; therefore all was well.

All *is* well if you can believe 2 Corinthians 12.9 or Luke 18.27. By believing the "I will" of the Lord Jesus, your problem is solved. Faith is not *asking* for what God has already promised. Faith is *believing* the promise of God.

Once a brother spoke on how to cross the threshold to victory. After he finished speaking, he opened the time for questions and answers. In the audience I saw a young sister with tears running down her cheeks, but she did not stand up and ask a

---

*Quoted verbatim from a later source than that which was available to the author in 1935. Passage found in Steven Barabas, *So Great Salvation* (Westwood, N.J.: Fleming H. Revell Company, 1957), p. 167.—*Translator*

question. However, an elderly sister nearby stood up and asked, "In these years I have always prayed for victory, yet I have never gotten the victory. What is the problem?" "Your problem is none other than praying too much," replied that brother. "All is well if you change your prayer to praise." As soon as the word was spoken, a brother stood up and said, "I have asked for victory for eleven years with no result. Now I have gotten it through listening to the question and answer between this elderly sister and you." The ministering brother then went over to the young sister and inquired how she was. "I too have gotten the victory after listening to the question and answer," responded the young sister. And such is faith.

Let us not take for granted that letting go, by itself, is victory. Without faith, you are still unable to substantiate God's fact. Just as the color in a painting needs to be substantiated by the eye, the sound of the organ by the ear, and the shape of a substance by the hand, so the promise and the word of God must be substantiated by faith. We do not pray, "O God, be my victory gradually, be my life gradually, or be my holiness gradually." No, we pray, "O God, You *are* my victory; I praise and thank You! O God, You *are* my life; I praise and thank You! O God, You *are* my holiness!"

I want you to know that I have encountered many temptations in my life. Many difficult problems have come my way; and many hard words have fallen upon my ears. Do I ask God to give me strength that I may overcome? On the contrary, I say, "O Lord, I praise and thank You, for You are my victory! O Lord, You overcome for me, and I praise and thank You. You resist for me, and I praise and thank You! O Lord, You are my head, I am Your member. You are the trunk, and I am a branch. You supply me with all I need." And I have found that He is already supplying all my needs according to His own word.

We each are perhaps saved by one verse out of the thousands to be found in God's word. Some are saved through John 3.16; others, through John 5.24; and still others, from Romans 10.10.

Just one word of God and a person is saved! This is also true with respect to victory. One out of the many words of God will bring a believer victory—even as that brother received the victory through the word of Jesus, "I will" (Matt. 8.3a). Many have entered into victory through 2 Corinthians 12.9, Romans 6.14, or 1 Corinthians 1.30.

Faith Is Not Hoping

All who are merely hoping may not have believed. If you ask a person whether he has overcome, and his answer is that he *hopes* to overcome, you know for sure that he does not have faith, even as you know a person does not have faith if he says he *hopes* to be saved. Some here are expecting all the time that the Lord will deliver them and cause them to overcome. Some here are praying continuously to the Lord asking for victory. Some are waiting a long while for the Lord to give them victory. Some may even claim that they have yielded and believed, but they are waiting to see if it works. It will never work if people wait to see whether or not it is effective, for faith is not hoping.

A brother once asked me if, after one has experienced victory, he must always remember that the Lord Jesus was his victory. Now it so happened that he supervised the jobs of over twenty employees in the factory where he himself was employed. And such supervision, he told me, occupied him from early morning till eight o'clock at night. How, then, he asked, could he possibly remember this matter all the time when he had to take care of so many things? Could he still overcome? I asked him in reply whether he continually remembered while at the factory that he had two eyes? Of course not, he answered. Did he need to touch his eyes with his hand after work to make sure they were still there? Certainly not, he replied. Therefore, I said to him, whether he remembered or not was unimportant because what was really essential was that the eyes were there. Praise and thank God, the victorious life in us does not depend on our remembrance of the Lord; rather, it depends on the Lord remembering us. How hard for us to always remember Him, but thank God, it is He who remembers us!

Faith Is Not Feeling

Some may not be hoping, praying or waiting; they may instead be on the lookout for feeling. One sister told me that although she had already yielded and had believed that the Lord was living in her, she dared not say she had overcome, because from the day she had accepted the victory of the Lord right up to the present moment, she had not felt anything. Let me emphasize the truth that faith is purely believing: it has no regard for feeling. Feeling may be useful in certain other things, but in knowing the Lord it is absolutely useless and untrustworthy. The hand can only touch and feel cold or hot, but it cannot see a painting. In spiritual matters, faith, and not feeling, is what is required to prove them. Victory is based on believing God's word. Because God has said so, so it is — and not because during these days you feel especially strong or joyful. Victory rests on one word of God.

One morning a brother came to tell me his problem. He had already yielded and believed, but he dared not say he had victory. Satan was accusing him all the time. Something had happened the other day, he told me, which made him doubt that his victory was real. It was clear to me he was trusting his feelings. So I spoke to him by means of a parable: I had a garden behind my house which I sold to you one day and gave you the deed to the property. As you went to the garden, a man suddenly appeared and said to you that one piece of the garden belonged to him. What were you to do? There were two alternatives available: either you would believe the deed I gave you which specified the extent of the entire garden, or you would believe that man's word. If my deed were true, then that man lied. Whom would you believe? Were you to believe the stranger's word, you

would have to let him stay in the garden. But if you believed
my word, you could order him to remove himself from your
property.

Now the promise and the word of God are wholly dependable. But were you to trust in your feelings and say that your
temper and pride were insoluble problems, then would not God's
word become untrustworthy? Yet if you believe in God's word,
all these problems you have would be solved.

God gives you a covenant specifying that gentleness, patience,
humility, love, self-control and whatever else is in Christ are all
yours. Nevertheless, you lose your temper, you become proud
and unclean, and you are defeated. What should you do? If you
believe God's word, you will say, "O God, I thank and praise
You, I am able to be gentle, patient, humble, loving, and in control of myself because Christ lives in me." By laying hold of God's
word, all the things you are afraid of will go away.

Unbelief Is the Greatest Sin

Today the greatest problem among the children of God is the
failure to believe His word. It may not be too difficult for them
to let go, and after letting go, believing ought to be fairly easy
too. Yet this is not the case.

I asked a sister who had let go and handed over everything
to the Lord if she had victory. Her reply was that she dared not
say she had. And why? Because she had not seen any result. So
I spoke to her directly: "You have committed the greatest sin of
mankind, which is unbelief. Your unbelief reflects on God as
though He were lying. For He has said that you are the branch,
and that if you let go, His life will live out from you. Yet you
are now saying that though you have let go, God has still not
delivered you. In short, you are saying *you* have done your duty,
but *God* has not fulfilled His responsibility." She denied that she
had had such intention. I therefore told her, "You should say,
'O God, I thank and praise You, for You have already given me
the victory.'"

You who believe that the Lord is head and that He is your life must observe *this* word from the Bible: "Believe that ye *received* them, and ye shall have them" (Mark 11.24b mg., Greek original). Believe, and the hardest shall pass away. Believe, then nothing can stand in your way to victory. This is salvation! Today our faith is not work; it is a substantiating God's fact. Believe that the Lord is head, believe that He lives in you, believe that He is your life, believe He is the trunk and you are the branch, and believe that He overcomes for you. Believe, and all temptations will fall away. Believe that all is done by the Lord. Praise and thank Him, for everything is done by Him!

What God has spoken is most trustworthy. We do not believe or trust in our experiences or feelings, but we do believe in the word of God. God says that the Lord Jesus not only died on the cross to be our righteousness but He now lives in us to be our sanctification. Therefore, we may not only say Christ is our righteousness but also say Christ is our sanctification. It is not that we *feel* that Christ is our life and sanctification, but that we believe He *is* our life and sanctification. God says Christ is our life, so we too say Christ is our life. God declares that Christ is our sanctification, therefore we also declare that Christ is our sanctification. God asserts that Christ is our victory, and hence we too assert that Christ is our victory. God says it, so we believe it.

I asked another sister in Chefoo if she had yielded. She replied that she *had* let go of herself, because God had said, "I have been crucified with Christ." I asked further if she knew victory, to which she answered that she dared not say so, because she had no assurance. I therefore spoke to her quite frankly: "Sister, God says that Christ is your life, but you say Christ may or may not be your life. God says Jesus Christ is your sanctification, yet you say He may or may not be your sanctification. God says His grace is sufficient for you, nevertheless you say God's grace may or may not be sufficient for you. Most surely one of you is lying. If God is right, you must be wrong; or vice versa. Now do you dare to say that God is a liar? Judging by what you have already said, are you not suggesting that God's word is untrustworthy?" Immediately her face changed color. She denied that she had made any such insinuation, for she *did* believe in God's word. She finally saw my point.

I would ask this of you: do you think it is a small matter if you continue to waver and hesitate about knowing Christ as your life and sanctification? Let me seriously warn you that you will be accusing God of lying.

I briefly asked still another sister in Chefoo if she had let go. Her answer was that she had. But did she have victory? She knew she lacked the victory because she still had some insignificant problems in her life. As I was pressed for time, I asked God to give me utterance to answer her. This was what I said to her: You say you have no faith, but in God's sight you have committed a great sin, the sin of not believing in His word. God has said to you that Christ is your life, your sanctification, and your victory. He has also told you that His grace is sufficient for you. But you do not believe, and you dismiss it with a smile as though it were of little consequence. Sister, let me tell you, you have committed a grave sin! You should go and pray: "O God, I do not believe in Your word. I have sinned against You. O God, forgive me, and take away my wicked heart of unbelief. Rid me of this my sin."

Someone may be unbelieving; yet, sad to say, he may deem it to be a trivial matter. In truth he has committed a great sin. This sin of unbelief is greater than the sin of adultery or murder. He should therefore pray, "O God, please forgive me, for I have sinned against You. Please take away from me this wicked heart of unbelief." If anyone considers his not believing in God's word to be sin, he will quickly cross over the threshold to victory. Faith is based on God's word, such a word as "My grace is sufficient for thee" (2 Cor. 12.9a) or that "Christ Jesus . . . was made unto us wisdom from God, both righteousness and sanctification and redemption (1 Cor. 1.30 mg.) or "Christ, who is our life" (Col. 3.4a). Lay hold of God's word, and all is well!

7 | The Testing of Faith

That the proof of your faith, being more precious than gold
that perisheth though it is proved by fire. (1 Peter 1.7a)

We will now turn to the testing of faith. The Scriptures show us that there is not a time when faith will not be tested. All faith must be proven. The reasons for the testing of faith are as follows:

1. That We May Grow. God tests our faith in order that we may grow. No Christian can advance without his faith being tested. Christians all over the world have their faith challenged. I have no reservation in making such a statement, because the only way for faith to grow is to have it proven. In leading us into growth, God uses the only method available: He allows our faith to go through testing. We come to God and accept His grace through faith. And hence, when our faith is tested, we just naturally grow.

2. That God's Heart May be Satisfied. God puts our faith to the test not only to cause us to grow but also to satisfy His own heart. No one in the world is exempt from having his faith tried after he has believed in the Lord and received God's grace. The reason for such testing is to prove that your faith is real. The realness of your faith in turn satisfies God's heart. Such tested faith glorifies

His name. Through whatever tribulation or persecution or opposition or darkness you are being tested, if you believe without faltering, then that faith of yours gives glory to God's name.

3. That the Mouth of Satan May Be Stopped. God causes our faith to go through testing not only to make us grow and to enable us to satisfy His heart, but also to stop Satan's mouth. God's enemy is deadly opposed to our saying that we have believed. He tries to hinder us from claiming that we have received in faith. He always throws doubts and troubles at us. But by testing our faith, God shuts up the mouth of Satan. For the latter discovers that we are no easy prey, and he will thus retreat. If possible, he will always attempt to hinder us from living peacefully and having the blessings of God. He will not give up till he himself is shut up. In order to shut the mouth of Satan, God must try our faith.

4. That We May Help Other People. Another reason why God tests our faith is to equip us for helping other people. One whose faith has not been tested is unable to help others. People can only receive help from the one whose faith has been proven. One's faith is undependable if he professes to have believed and yet his faith has not been tried. But a truly tested faith renders Satan helpless; and such faith helps the whole church.

Unquestionably, a faith that has been tested and proven is more precious than gold (1 Peter 1.7).

The Relationship between Faith Tested and Victory

The reason for the testing of our faith is to show us what faith really is. Genuine faith is long-lived. Whatever is short-lived is not faith. Genuine faith is that which can believe after days or months or years. It is able to endure obstacles once and many times over. It will continue to believe after being tested to the seventh time. A so-called short-lived faith that is terminated after one encounter with difficulty is no faith at all.

The Scriptures show us that victory comes through believing the word of God. God has said that His Son is our life, our head, our victory, our sanctification, our power. And we know that He bears all our burdens, takes care of all our responsibilities, supplies us with patience and gentleness, and supports us from within. Thank and praise the Lord! We believe and we know. Such faith nonetheless will have to be tested.

This morning, one brother said to me, "I have let go, I have believed, I have crossed the threshold of victory. But yesterday after the meeting while I was returning home on my bicycle, I was hit by an elderly man and fell from the bicycle. At that time, though I did not say anything outwardly, inwardly my temper had already risen. What about this? I have let go, confessed my inability, believed that Christ is my victory, but my temper heated up even though I was not thinking of losing my temper. What is this?" Quite simply, this is due to two factors:

1. Our Victory Does Not Mean We Have Changed. Having crossed the threshold of victory, we may think we have changed and improved when afterwards we did not sin for a few weeks. We begin to be elated, even to boast of our achievement. Whereupon God decides to test us, allowing us to fail so as to make us realize that we have not changed one iota for the better. The reason for our newly-found patience is not because we have changed, but because Christ is patient for us. If we consider ourselves changed, we will undoubtedly fall. We ought to know that we can be patient only because Christ is our patience, we can only be gentle because Christ is our gentleness, we can only be holy because He is our holiness. Even after we have overcome for many days, we remain the same, we are forever ourselves, and we have not changed one whit. Watchman Nee is forever Watchman Nee. After fifty years, he will still be Watchman Nee. Take away grace, and Watchman Nee remains Watchman Nee. I thank and praise the Lord! Victory is Christ; it has nothing to do with me. I am still able to sin; I have not changed at all.

In Chefoo some missionaries asked me what change was, and what exchange was. I replied: "Paul plus Peter plus John minus grace is equal to sinners. This is not only true of Paul, Peter and John; it is true with us 'common' people as well. Apart from the grace of God, we are no different from the robbers and prostitutes. If there is grace present, then it is Christ substituting for us and not because we have changed." How true is the word in a hymn, "Whene'er my heart is lifted up, how very near I am to fall" (R. H. Earnshaw). Let us ever keep in mind that you and I are still the same; we have not changed at all.

2. Which Is Trustworthy — the Word of God or Our Experience? How easily we believe and trust in our experience. We reckon that people so weak and defeated and ill-tempered as we are are in no position for victory. This is because we look at our own experience and consider God's word to be false. But let me ask you, which is trustworthy— the word of God or your own experience?

In Chefoo, a sister came to see me. She confessed that she had yielded and fully believed Christ as her victory, yet her victory was rather short-lived; it lasted but one week. A week later, two of her children quarreled with each other, and she could endure no longer. During the last three days she told me she had had no victory at all. "What is wrong?" she asked. I inquired of her if Christ had changed. She replied, no. Then had the word of God changed? I asked. Again she answered, no. Since neither Christ nor God's word had changed, how could she say she had had no victory? Her reply: because she could endure no more.

So at this point I used a parable: Suppose your son meets a man on the street who says to him, "Young man, you are not born of your mother. Rather, your mother bought you at the drugstore for twenty cents." Suppose your son then runs home and asks you, "Mother, am I born by you or was I bought by

you at the drugstore for twenty cents? I ask you this because a
stranger I met on the street just now told me I was bought." You
say to your son, "Son, you are born of me. Do not believe what
the stranger said."

He leaves you and meets another person who tells him the
same thing, with the additional word that he was an eyewitness
at the scene of the purchase. Again, your son comes home to
ask you about this new word. So you say to your son, "What!
You still do not believe *my* word?" Once more your boy goes out
and meets the same man who asks him if he has asked his mother
once again about it. And then the man adds that on the day of
the transaction at the drugstore, not only *he* had been there, but
about twenty *other* persons could serve as witnesses too!

At this point I said to the sister in Chefoo that on the one
hand was the mother's word, and the mother's word needed no
witness; on the other hand was the word of the stranger, and
he had many false witnesses. I then asked the sister, "Who would
the son believe — the mother's word that needed no proof, or the
stranger's word that was full of false evidence? Were your son
to come back and still ask you whether he was born by you or
bought by you, you would most certainly say to him, 'You, little
child, are really a fool!'

"Likewise, sister, today, God will say to you that you are a
foolish child! For He has made His Son your holiness, life and
victory. God said, and it was done. Moreover, He has said it again
and again in His word. But you grow anxious and say: 'Something
is wrong, because I have proofs that I have not overcome.
Although God has said that His Son is my holiness, I say I am
proven to have no holiness.'

"Let me ask you, what is the difference between your behavior
here and that of the son in the parable? You have believed in
Satan's lie which is full of false evidence, and you do not declare
the word of God. Were some man to actually come to your son
to deceive him, I tell you without reservation that your son would

smilingly respond that his mother's word was most trustworthy and the stranger was a liar. And thus would your son put the enemy to shame but would glorify his mother.

"Let me tell you here and now that if Satan comes to make you feel cold, weak and defeated, you should say, 'I am victorious, for Christ is my victory.' If he comes to make you feel hasty, you still should say, 'I am victorious, because Christ is my victory.' By so doing you declare that what Satan does and says is a lie, because only the word of God is true. This is faith, and such tested faith is the kind which glorifies God's name.

"If you confess with your mouth that you believe, and yet the moment you are tempted you return home crying, where is your faith? Such faith is short-lived, for genuine faith must go successfully through testing. You are finished if as soon as you encounter temptation you concede you do not have victory."

When you are faced with temptation, you will stand victoriously if you declare that God's word — the word of Jehovah of hosts — is trustworthy and dependable. Whatever God says is yea and amen, and His word is set in heaven forever. The question now is, whose word will you believe?

Where Faith Is, the Mountain Is Removed

To another sister who had a similar problem I said that we must have faith that removes the mountain (see Matt. 17.20, 21.21; Mark 11.23; 1 Cor. 13.2). Whatever succumbs to temptation is not faith. What is meant by the faith which removes the mountain? A faith that is firm and unyielding is called the faith which removes a mountain. Such faith is not blocked by any obstacle. Where such belief is, difficulty is moved away. Mountain and faith do not co-exist. Either the mountain is removed or the faith is removed. Each testing is for the sake of removing the mountain. Therefore, the question now is not in relation to the matter of testing, but rather in relation to what is removed — the mountain or faith? whether we believe in the word of the stranger or in the word of God? That which fails the testing is not genuine faith.

One brother professed he had crossed the threshold of victory and yet he did not see victory. Satan insinuated that he was cheated, for there was no such thing as victory. Well, if you say you are cheated, you are finished, because God will do to you according to what you believe.

I recall how on one occasion I was sick in my room upstairs in this very building where I am now. A brother took my temperature and pulse. The temperature was feverish, and the pulse beat fast. For several nights I had no sleep. I was near the gate of death. During that particular night I prayed, and the next morning I had the word of the Lord that He had heard my prayer. He gave me Romans 8.11: "if the Spirit of him that raised up Jesus from the dead dwelleth in you, he that raised up Christ Jesus from the dead shall give life also to your mortal bodies through his Spirit that dwelleth in you." I thought I would surely sleep well that night, not knowing that it was actually going to be even worse that night.

The next day this same brother came to take my temperature and pulse again. My fever rose higher and my pulse beat faster. Satan was most diligent. He instantly hinted to me as to what kind of promise really *was* it? For I had been promised by God to be quickened and revived and yet I did not look as though I were going to live. Satan's mocking word seemed reasonable. Yet just at that moment, God immediately gave me two more Scripture verses: one was in Jonah 2.8 —"They that regard lying vanities forsake their own mercy." This was the word spoken by Jonah when in the fish's belly. My outward circumstances were all lying vanities. Another verse was John 17.17b —"Thy word is truth." God says that His word is truth; all other words are falsehoods.

If God's word is truth, then my feverish temperature, my runaway pulse, and even my sleepless night were all falsehoods. I therefore thanked God at once, declaring that the word in

Romans 8.11 was still true while all my symptoms were false. Thus I believed, and thus I declared. In the afternoon my fever receded and my pulse slowed down. I also was able to sleep that night. This is the testing of faith, and this is the removal of the mountain.

Genuine Faith Believes in God's Word Alone

What is genuine faith? Genuine faith believes in the word of God exclusively, it is not believing in one's own experience, feeling, or dark environment. If environment and experience coincide with God's word, we praise and thank the Lord. But if these disagree with His word, then the word of God alone stands true. Whatever is contrary to God's word is false. Satan may insinuate to you, saying: How can you say you have victory? Where is your victory since you are as corrupt and weak as you were before? But you can counter him with this: "Indeed, I am still I, I will never change, but God says Christ is my holiness, my life and my victory." Though Satan suggests that you are still corrupt and weak, God's word remains true. Whatever the enemy whispers to you is false; only the word of the Lord is true!

In Chefoo, I learned a lesson. One day, Miss Elizabeth Fischbacher* and I were praying especially for gifts. I asked for the gift of faith, and she asked for the gift of healing. We prayed for only about fifteen minutes, believing we had received the gifts. In the evening we went to the meeting. Sister Hu told us that the sister who lived in the room below the meeting hall was mentally deranged. Previously, she had turned schizophrenic once or twice a month, but recently she had often shown signs of mental derangement. The meeting ended at ten thirty. As I returned home, I was thinking what should be done for the person who lived in the room below the meeting hall and was mentally sick.

---

*Miss Fishbacher was from Scotland, a missionary in China for many years, and a much respected fellow worker of Watchman Nee.—*Translator*

After I parted company with a brother, the word of God immediately came to me: "the proof of your faith, being more precious than gold that perisheth though it is proved by fire" (1 Peter 1.7). I said to myself, "Fine, faith was now to be tested."

So the following day I went to find sister Fischbacher. I could have dealt with the case alone, but because yesterday she had received the gift of healing and I had received the gift of faith, we should now put them to use. When sister Fischbacher heard that I had invited her to go with me, she was slightly taken aback. She said she would pray about it. After praying, she decided to go with me. When we arrived, the patient had just fallen asleep. So the physician, Dr. Shih, suggested that we wait till she woke up, but added that humanly speaking this was a hopeless case. Now it so happened that sister Fischbacher had to be on board a boat that left at 11:30. We waited till 10:50 before we were asked to go in.

I spoke a few words to the patient. I noticed that her hair began to stand up, which indicated she was going to become mad. But praise and thank God, I prayed for a minute or two, and the Lord gave me faith. As faith arose within me, I commenced to praise God. At that moment I knew she would get well. Sister Fischbacher also prayed a few words, and she too had faith. So she also praised God. Two brothers and one sister who accompanied us also prayed, but they evidently were not in the flow of the Holy Spirit. The time was up for sister Fischbacher to depart, so we left to see her off.

When I came back from the pier to see the patient, she was crying and laughing and "raising hell." After a while, she fainted. None knew what to do. At that very moment, I came to know what was meant by faith being tested. Dr. Shih took me out of the room and suggested that I pray immediately, for he as a doctor could not do anything. I said there was no need to pray. I smilingly challenged Satan to try his best. The patient was mad and I looked mad too. She was "raising hell" *inside* the room, and I was storming hell *outside* the room. She *raged* for three and a half hours, while I *smiled* for three and a half hours. During that period, my faith really rose up. There would be a meeting at 4:00 o'clock which I had to attend. As I left, I told Dr. Shih: "Do not be anxious, nor think of doing anything. Let Satan exhaust his power. What God says, that is so. For the Lord never plays a trick on us."

In the evening, Dr. Shih told me the patient was getting better. The next morning, Dr. Shih told me she was almost normal. I knew, however, she would rant and rave again because the faith of a few other brethren would now have to be tested.

In the afternoon, she did indeed rant and rave again. Dr. Shih came and asked me what should be done. I knelt to pray, but no word came, and faith seemed not to rise. At that moment, Satan was extremely busy. Mockingly, the enemy hinted, "Why not smile again? You smiled yesterday; why not smile today?" It seemed I had lost my faith. But thank and praise God, there was a voice within me saying, "Your feeling did change today from yesterday, for you could smile yesterday but today you feel frigid. However, I *the Lord* have not changed." I said to myself, "Indeed, the Lord has *not* changed." At once I broke out in praise: "Lord, You have *not* changed." Yesterday I believed in God's word; yet my smile on that day could not make God any the *more* trustworthy. Today my feeling was cold, yet neither could it cause God's faithfulness to be any the *less* trustworthy. I therefore thanked the Lord and prayed no more.

In the evening, Dr. Shih reported to me that according to medical diagnosis the patient could be declared fully well. On the next day, even her facial color had changed for the better. Hallelujah, the word of God *is* trustworthy. This was the testing of faith.

Oh! How we expect to see a result as soon as we believe! We want to experience victory the very moment we believe. But let me ask you if you can believe God for three hours, three days, even three months. If you cannot believe Him for three hours, three days or three months, where is your faith? "He that believeth shall not be in haste" (Is. 28.16b).

One evening the Lord commanded His disciples to cross the Lake of Galilee to the other side. Suddenly there arose a great storm of wind, and the waves beat upon the boat so much that it was now filling up. The Lord Jesus was in the stern, asleep on a cushion. The disciples awakened Him and said, "Teacher, carest thou not that we perish?" The Lord arose and rebuked the wind. But what did He say to His disciples immediately afterwards? In the Gospel according to Mark, Jesus is recorded as saying: "have ye not yet faith?" (4.40) In the Gospel according to Matthew the record reads: "O ye of little faith" (8.26). This indicates that many hasty prayers are but an expression of unbelief. If there were faith, you would stand firm. The Lord orders you to cross to the other side; He has not commanded you to go to the bottom of the lake. Because He has given His order—and no matter how strong the wind blows or how high the waves beat—the boat *cannot* capsize. People with little or no faith hide themselves as soon as they are faced with obstacles. With *genuine* faith, you can meet the test headlong and stand. Little faith hides at testing, whereas big faith stands against the testing. False faith falls in trial, but genuine faith stands throughout all the trial.

Stand on the Side of Faith

On one occasion a person began to scold me severely. The more I endured, the more he scolded. I asked God at that time, "O God, please quickly give me patience and strength so that I may be able to endure; otherwise, I will hastily lose my temper." If this were to happen again today, not only am I unafraid but I can also smilingly say, "Satan, you may use that person to berate me even more strongly. Yet see if you can upset the Christ in me." I will not hate the person who reviles me; I can even love him. And if this is so, what can the enemy possibly do? Praise and thank God, victory is Christ, not I. Were it I, I could only endure so much, and then I would explode. But if it be Christ, no temptation will be too much for Him, nor any testing too difficult for Him. Stand on the side of God's word, stand on the side of faith—and Satan is rendered helpless. Since the Lord orders us to go to the other side, to the other side we will go. Not because *our* word counts, but because God's word is trustworthy, for He is forever faithful.

In conclusion, let me ask you if you are frightened by one or two old sins? I suppose you must have a problem like that. But I will further ask you: when the Christ who dwells in you allows you to be tested, who is the one really being tested? Permit me to say to you that each time a trial of faith comes your way, do understand that it is not you being proven, it is the Lord. When your faith is being proven, it is the Son of God being proven; it is God's faithfulness and not you that is being tested. For whatever trial descends upon you, it is to test what Christ can do. Each trial tests the faithfulness of God. By standing on the side of God and His word, by standing on the side against feeling and environment, you have faith—and this can truly be called victory. Satan says you are still unclean, but you can say Christ is my holiness. Satan says you are yet proud, but you can say Christ is my humility. Satan says you are still defeated, but you can say Christ is my victory. No matter what the enemy says, your response is and always shall be that Christ is trustworthy and God's word is dependable. This is faith; this substantiates the truthfulness of God's word. Hallelujah, Christ overcomes, God is still faithful, and His word remains altogether trustworthy!

Remember that the trying of faith will not be long. During the period when you first cross the threshold of victory, you will be especially tested. However, once having your faith tested, you will be able to help and benefit other people. God's heart will be satisfied, and his name will be glorified. Satan's mouth will be sealed, and he can do nothing to you. Praise the Lord, the word of God is trustworthy! Thank God, that when you stand before Him, nothing can stand before you. When you stand in faith, there is no mountain that cannot be removed, because faith is for the sake of removing mountains. If there be a mountain in your path, it shall be removed indeed.

8 | Growth

Sanctify them in the truth: thy word is truth. (John 17.17)

Before proceeding further in our discussion, let us review what we have already covered. We have seen that our experience is continuous defeat, but the life God has ordained for Christians is far superior to our experience. For the God-given life that wins is Christ. Our own ways of suppression, struggle, prayers and so forth are totally ineffective. We have also seen that of the five characteristics of the nature of this victorious life the most basic one is *exchange*, not change. The way to enter into this life is quite simple: yielding, which is letting go; and believing. God declares His grace is sufficient for us; therefore, it *is* sufficient. God declares that Christ is our life; and so, He *is* our life. God declares that Christ is our holiness; accordingly, He *is* our holiness. Then we explained more fully the meaning of letting go. We also mentioned that believing is but to substantiate that which God has already accomplished. Such faith, however, must go through testing.

Now we will deal with this matter of growth in connection with victory. How do we really grow? Perhaps after receiving the above messages, we might conclude that, having crossed the threshold to victory, our life surely has reached its summit to which nothing more can be added. It is because of this faulty conclusion that we should discuss what we must daily do if we have indeed entered into victory.

1. Overcome the Sin That Entangles Us. Many Christians after they have crossed the threshold to victory by knowing that Christ is their victory, do not know how to maintain it; thus they fall back again. First and foremost after a Christian has obtained the victory, he must expect and see God deliver him from that particular sin which always entangles and hinders him (see Heb. 12.1).

No one who has crossed the threshold may carry on with his special sin. The Lord has already delivered you. He is your life that wins. You may therefore pray, "O God, I thank and praise You, the victory of Christ is my victory. The holiness of Christ is my holiness." For it is Christ who lives in you. If you have a hot temper, your hot temper is gone. If you are troubled by unbelief or talkativeness or any of the eight kinds of sin we mentioned before, you can expect God to eliminate it. As soon as you enter into victory, you should say to the Lord, "O Lord, I expect You to overcome that special sin."

Of course, there are many sins which need to be dealt with. If, for example, you have sinned against someone or your brother, you should go to him and apologize. Formerly you did not have the courage to apologize, now you have the strength to do so. Or you might be bound by a certain thing in the past, but now because Christ lives in you, you shall be set free. Hence every brother or sister must expect God to rid him or her of his or her special sin — the entangling sin of the past — soon after he or she obtains the life that wins. In the event you allow that special sin to remain in your life, not only brothers and sisters cannot believe you have overcome, even you yourself will doubt it. Before you receive the life that wins, you have no strength to fight; but now possessing that life, you have the strength to overcome. Now you have faith to win.

In Chefoo, some missionaries asked me this: would there be

no fighting upon once having entered into victory? My answer was: Do you fight *to* victory or fight *from* victory? If you fight *to* victory, you will never succeed. But if you fight *from* victory, you are on the right track.

Many are always striving with much effort for victory, but they usually end up in defeat. For victory is not attained through men's own effort; victory is dependent wholly on Christ and is wholly given by God. You have believed that the Lord is your holiness, perfection and victory. Consequently, all these sins must go away—"Every plant which my heavenly Father planted not, shall be rooted up" (Matt. 15.13).

In my speaking with a brother about this matter I used an example: Suppose you bought a piece of land, and the seller gave you the deed which specified the length and width of the property. When you went to assume ownership of the land, you learned that some rogues had insisted upon building a hut on your property to dwell there. What will you now do? You will drive out these rogues on the basis of what was written in the deed. Just so is our fight with sin. We do not fight by our own power; we fight by the authority which God has given us. True, the Bible says we ought to fight, but it says we fight *with faith*. When the Bible says we must overcome the enemy, it means we overcome by faith. We resist the devil with "the shield of faith" (Eph. 6.16a).

Let me ask you, is your hot temper included in the life of Christ? Your unbelief, talkativeness or whatever the special sin that entangles you — does it belong to the life of Christ? You and I know these do *not* belong to Him. Since they are not Christ's, you can command them to be removed. If you think of resisting to the point of victory, you will invariably fail. If you use your own strength to fight to victory, you will also fail. But if you resist and fight because you have the victory already, you will always prevail. Hence the all-important question is this—do you fight *to* victory or fight *from* victory? In the event that you fight *from* victory, you will pray, "O God, I thank and praise You because

Christ has already overcome! Since *He* has overcome, all these sins will be driven out." Every Christian once crossing the threshold to victory should declare that the special sin must leave because Christ is his life. The sin which entangles you is put out with the little push of faith—and this is called victory.

2. Acknowledge Our Own Inability and Accept Christ As All. Your life each day must be the same as it was on the very first day you crossed the threshold of victory. Each morning upon getting up you will pray, "O God, I am before You as unable and feeble and unchanged as before. But, God, I thank you because You are still my life, my holiness and my victory. I believe during the entire day ahead You will live out Your life in me. I praise and thank You, for all is Your grace, all is done by Your Son."

Yet there are a few things to which you need to pay attention, and these will be discussed below.

Two Kinds of Temptation and the Ways of Dealing with Them

Let us recall that brother mentioned earlier who was knocked off his bicycle while cycling home after a meeting. It so happened that he was not even thinking of losing his temper, yet he exploded. If there had been time to reflect, he might have been able to suppress his temper. But what happened to him did not give him the opportunity to think. Let me therefore observe that the temptations which we daily encounter are of two kinds: one sort of temptation comes suddenly upon us and gives no time; another sort comes slowly to us through progressive suggestions. One kind gives us no time to reflect; the other gives us time to consider. We agree that it is easier to overcome temptation which gives us time to think than it is to overcome temptation which gives us *no* time to reflect. In view of this, then once we have crossed the threshold of victory, we need to pray concerning these two things every morning; otherwise, we shall fall.

First, we should say to the Lord, "O Lord, deliver me in the midst of temptations which give me no time to reflect, so that I may not sin." The Lord will enable you to overcome such unexpected temptations. Such prayer is most precious. It has delivered many souls.

We have no time to consider the entire fifth chapter of Romans; I will simply comment a little about it here. Romans 5.12-19 teaches us that our union with Christ is similar to our union with Adam. Previously, we sinned because we were joined to Adam; now we practice righteousness because we are joined to Christ. For example, how many of us have to exert any effort to blow up? None, obviously, because we know that our temper flares up just as soon as it is touched by the slightest provocation. Due to the union with Adam, our losing our temper is most natural. Our union with Adam results in sinning without the need of any resolve or effort on our part to bring it about. Yet this is also true with regard to the life in Christ promised to us by God. You should say to the Lord, "As I previously had been united with Adam so that I could sin without any resolve or pondering, so today I am in Christ in order that I may be patient, kind, or whatever without any resolve, pondering, or resisting on my part. O Lord, though I have no time to reflect, yet I praise and thank You that my union with Christ is as deep as that union was with Adam. Accordingly, when temptation comes to me today, and even if it gives me no time to reflect or resist, You have already manifested Your gentleness, holiness, and victory through me."

If you stand before God on that position, you will overcome this first kind of temptation. As you rise up in the morning, you believe that God will deliver you from temptation which gives you no time to think. Each morning you believe that the life of

Christ will live out His victory when you are unconscious of it. The question is therefore reduced to this matter of faith. All the facts of God will become your experience if you believe.

Second, regarding the other kind of temptation which does not arrive suddenly but rather slowly and persistently, what should you do about it? Do not resist, simply ignore it. The whole issue is centered upon Christ. You have not changed; you are still weak and have no power to resist. You cannot and you will not. As you were unable before, you are still unable now. You simply raise your head and look at the Lord in prayer, acknowledging that He is able, because He is not weak but is all powerful in you. Stand into this position, and the temptation will flee. When you try to strive and resist, the temptation seems unwilling to leave you. But when you say you cannot but God can, when you glory in His power as well as in your weakness, the temptation immediately vanishes.

The Just Shall Live by Faith

Some brothers have asked if they will never sin again once they have crossed the threshold to victory. My answer is, eventually we shall arrive at such a place, but we still have the possibility of sinning. What kind of living do the Scriptures show us? They unveil the fact that the Christian life is one of faith: "the righteous shall live by faith" (Rom. 1.17b).

There are two realms before us: one is the physical world, the other is the spiritual world. With our five senses, we live in the first; with our faith we live in the second. When viewing yourself from your own vantage point, you readily acknowledge you are yet a sinner, unclean and proud, as is the rest of the world. But when viewing yourself in Christ with the eye of faith, you realize your hot temper and hardness are all gone. The problem today is that you must choose daily between these two realms. We human beings are rational, emotional, and volitional in our constitution. Our will is free to choose either of these two worlds, and the one we choose shall be the world we live in. If you rely on the five senses and thereby live in the physical world, you will manifest this world in your life. But if by faith you live in the spiritual world, you will express in your life the spiritual world. In other words, when you are governed by your mind, your feelings and your self-will, you immediately live in Adam; but when you are governed by faith you instantly live in Christ. You are torn between these two polarities: if you rely on feeling, you live in Adam, but if you rely on faith you live in Christ. And when you live in Christ, all that is in Him becomes your experience.

The Bible does not teach the doctrine of the eradication of sin. Yet according to God's work and provision and command, no believer should practice sin. We ought to manifest Christ daily, and we should be more than conquerors daily. Nonetheless, the moment we live in our feelings, we fall. We should instead live daily in faith, and thus shall we substantiate all that is in Christ.

Immediately Restored by the Blood After Failure

If we unfortunately fail, however, what should we do? We may at once come to God and lay our sin under the precious blood of Christ. In the very next second, we may look at Heaven and say: "O God, I thank and praise You, Your Son is still my life and my holiness. And Your Son shall live out His victorious life through me." We can be restored in a few seconds. We do not need to wait for five minutes or an hour. Oftentimes, God has already forgiven us and cleansed us from our sins, yet we think we ought to suffer and be punished a little longer so that our sin may be cleansed better. This is making trouble for ourselves. It is still living by feeling, thus living in Adam.

Perhaps someone will ask if *after* victory there are still failures which require the cleansing of the precious blood? In view of this question, we need first to inquire as to what, if any, is the difference between the time before and after entering into victory. Let me say that there is a vast difference! Before you crossed the threshold of victory, your life was a defeated one. You may have overcome occasionally, but defeat was more your norm. Upon crossing the threshold, however, your life became a victorious one. You may indeed sometimes fail today, yet you are always victorious. Formerly, there were more defeats, few victories; now though, there are less defeats, more victories. Previously, defeat was the rule. Your temper was always bad, your thoughts were always unclean, your attitude was always hard, and your nature was always jealous. You were usually bound by these sins, with victory quite rare. But now that you have obtained victory, your failure has become infrequent. Even when you fail today, you are not permanently bound by that sin.

Before victory, you were perplexed after having failed because you did not know how to be restored to the fellowship and the light of God. It seemed as though you had to climb a thousand steps, which was more than you could possibly do. *After* victory, however, you can today be restored in a few seconds following defeat. You immediately confess your sin, instantly get cleansed by the precious blood, and at once you are able to thank and praise God, because Christ lives out His victory through you again. And such is the difference between the two.

Maintain a Proper Relationship with Christ Daily

"The witness is this, that God gave unto us eternal life, and this life is in his Son. He that hath the Son hath the life; he that hath not the Son of God hath not the life" (1 John 5.11–12). How is this life that wins given to us? It is done so in the Son. There can be no victorious life without the Son. Whoever has the Son of God has the life; whoever does not have the Son of God does not have the life. It is not merely that God gives life to us; He gives this life to us *in the Son*. To receive this life that wins, we receive the Son of God, not simply receive life. For this reason, whenever our relationship with Christ becomes strained, our life is confronted with a problem. The moment we doubt as to the faithfulness of Christ and His promise, we fail in our life. For God has not given us patience, gentleness and humility; He has instead given us all these in His Son. If our relationship with God's Son becomes abnormal, our victory is instantly lost. We therefore need to maintain a proper relationship with Christ daily.

Let us say to the Lord each day, "O Lord, You are still my head, and I am still a member of Your body. You are my life and my holiness." If you turn your eyes upon yourself, you lose sight of these realities. But if your eyes are fixed on Christ, you have all these facts in experience. And this is what faith is all about. You cannot lay hold of holiness, victory, patience and humility outside of Christ. But *having* Christ you *have* holiness, victory, patience and humility. A Chinese proverb says: Take care of the green mountain, and you have no fear of a lack of wood for fuel. Figuratively speaking, God has not given us wood; He has given us our green mountain which is Christ. As long as this mountain exists, the wood supply of holiness, patience and so forth will just naturally exist and be ours. Hence, by daily believing in the Son of God who lives in us, we have all these things in our daily experience. A principle reason for the defeat of many Christians is because they live by feeling instead of living by faith.

In the event of defeat, it is not because the past experience is untrustworthy, but because faith is missing. Never accept the thought that we *need* to fail after victory. *Before* victory, we did need to fail. God permitted us to fail and to fail deeply, that we might know our own powerlessness. But *after* we know victory, failure is not necessary. And failure becomes incidental when it does occur. *In Adam*, we feel cold, lifeless, hard and unclean; and so we are what we *feel*. Today *in Christ*, however, we declare we *have* holiness, gentleness and victory; and thus we have these things in experience.

Grow through Seeing the Truth and Accepting Grace

Let us now see what real growth is. We *should* grow after we have victory. Yet some may boast that all is well now that they have gotten the victory. They may indeed have the victory. Without passing through the gate, one cannot walk down the road. But they should know that they have only crossed the threshold, they as it were have only passed through the gate. Only after victory is there the possibility of advancement and growth. Yet we can only manifest victory over the sins we already know, not the sins that we do not know. Hence with regard to the latter sins growth is absolutely necessary.

As regards the particular sin you already know about, let us suppose you have a hot temper. Once knowing the victory that is in Christ, your patience has become so perfect that it cannot be improved. And why? Because this perfect patience is Christ himself imparted to you. The patience you now have is exactly the same as the patience of Christ exhibited in His thirty-three and a half years' walk on the earth. Unless your patience is false, true patience is Christ your patience; therefore, this patience of yours today cannot be more patient. And thus you have manifested the victory of Christ over this particular sin you already knew.

Yet there are sins of which we are not conscious, and the victory in Christ has not been manifested over these sins. We therefore need the word of John 17 in regard to these sins: "Sanctify them [Christ's followers] in truth" (v.17a). On the one side is 1 Corinthians 1.30 which tells us that "Christ Jesus . . . was made unto us wisdom from God, both righteousness and sanctification and redemption" (mg.); on the other side is John 17.17a—"Sanctify them in the truth." What sanctifies us in holiness is Christ; what expands our *capacity* for holiness is the truth. Who understands the entire Bible? No one. We all come to understand it gradually. Truth tells us what is right and what is wrong.

So that many things we did not previously know to be sinful, we today consider to be so. Matters in our lives we did not reckon as sins two weeks ago we now realize *are* sinful. Even things in the more distant past we thought to be good we today look upon as sinful.

Why is there this difference between the present and the past? Because the more we understand the truth, the more sins are discovered. And the more we discover sins in our lives the more we need Christ as our very life. So that as the capacity for uncovering sins increases, the need to have Christ also increases more and more. Day by day let us read the word of God carefully so that we may know what is sinful. The more sins we discover, the more we will ask God to show us how Christ is our victory and supply in these areas. Hence the light of the truth is absolutely essential to our growth, for the light of the truth will expose our many faults and our uselessness. As the light of the truth reveals our actual situation, our capacity is thereby enlarged. And the larger the capacity, the more the absorption of Christ to be our very life.

I like very much the word in 2 Peter 3: "grow in the grace and knowledge of our Lord and Saviour Jesus Christ" (v.18a). This is the only place in the entire Bible where growth is mentioned. It is a growing in the grace. No beliver grows *into* grace, it is always growing *in* the grace.

Now grace means that God does for me. So to "grow in the grace" means I need God to do more for me. Five things He has already done for me, yet there are three more things I will need Him to do for me. As my need increases, I need God to do more for me. Such is the relation between grace and truth. Truth points out my lack, and grace supplies my need. Truth shows where I am lacking, and grace replenishes the lack. Hallelujah, God is not only the truth, He is also the grace! The people in the time of the Old Covenant always failed because they had the truth but not the grace. They had the law, yet they did not have the power to keep the law. We thank and praise God that though "the law was given through Moses; grace and truth came through Jesus Christ" (John 1.17). We today have the truth to unveil and the grace to supply.

Hereafter you may come to God and pray: "O God, I am forever a beggar. Today I come for my need; tomorrow and the day after tomorrow I will come again for my need. Thank God, I have need every day." If you come to Him in this manner, you will grow in grace. Time and again you see your failure, so time and again you ask God for more. You acknowledge you are helpless, therefore you need Him to be responsible for you. You need Him to be more and more responsible for you. Just as soon as you are conscious of your fault, the first thing you do is to pray, "O God, I confess my sin. Once more I learn a lesson. I can never be changed, and I am not going to try to change myself. O God, I thank You, once again I glory in my weakness. I thank You, that because You are able, You can take away my weakness." Each time you glory in your weakness, each time the power of Christ will overshadow you. Every time you say you cannot, every time God manifests *His* might. By continually doing this, you will constantly grow.

As we have said, there are many sins we are not conscious of, but as we come to know them through the truth of God's word, let us tell God immediately that we have sinned and that we need Christ to live out His life for us. Allow me to give a testimony at this point. After a person did me some wrong, I uttered a few hasty words to him. I knew I should not say these words, yet I argued that since he had wronged me so gravely and had not apologized to me, why should I conduct myself towards him without fault? Nevertheless, God wanted me to apologize. I did not hate the person who had wronged me. As a matter of fact, I had forgiven him. Still, I needed to confess my sin. I figured I was not too bad, yet I was unable to do what the light of truth in Matthew 5 revealed to me I should do: "Love your enemies" (v.44a). I reasoned that if I could love *him*, I could love anybody. Actually, I had composed a letter in which I had apologized to him for my hasty words. Now, though, I realized I could not love. So I could not send off that letter. I certainly could not write him until I could love him. I did not hate him; in fact, I had forgiven him; but I could not love him. Only God could. For God says love is truth; therefore not to love is a sin. I now wanted to overcome. I must fight the fight of faith. So I told God that unless He caused me to love, I could not love. One day I could honestly say I could not. And one day I could also truly say that God could. And on *that* day, I *could* love him. So that on the one hand truth says we should love; on the other hand, grace supplies us with the power to love. In dealing with such matters as this that I have just mentioned, sometimes a mere second will do; at other times, it may take several days.

Miss Fischbacher had a fellow worker who continually troubled her with all kinds of harassment. Whenever sister Fischbacher would say there was such and such a thing, she would say there was no such thing; or if Miss Fischbacher said there was no such thing, this fellow worker would say just the opposite. She seemed persistently to try to discredit Miss Fischbacher before men. Our sister tried to be patient with the fellow worker, but was at a loss as to how to deal with the situation. Each time she saw this fellow worker, she showed kindness by patting the latter's shoulder or by shaking hands with her. Outwardly, all appeared well, but inwardly something was amiss.

One day sister Fischbacher read the truth of 1 Peter 1.22: "Seeing ye have purified your souls in your obedience to the truth unto unfeigned love of the brethren, love one another from the heart fervently." She said to herself that she did not even love her fellow worker, how much less, then, could she love her fervently? So she prayed, "O God, I have no victory over this matter. I have found out that it is a sin. You say I must love the brethren fervently, but I cannot." She asked God to deliver her from this sin.

She did not hate, yet she could not love. Each time she met her fellow worker, she tried her best to love, but this was impossible. One day she shut herself in her room and confessed: "O God, I should love her, but I cannot. This is sin. If I cannot love her today, what will happen to me?" She prayed for three hours until the love of Christ filled her heart. At that moment, she could have even died for that sister. She not only loved her, but now she loved her fervently. With such fervent love in her heart, she prayed for her fellow worker the whole night. The next day in the afternoon after work, sister Fischbacher prayed for that sister again. And as a result, this fellow worker came through into victory and power.

Now this is an example of what is meant by John 17 —"sanctify them in the truth" (v.17a). This is what is meant by growing in the grace. Truth causes you to see sin, and grace supplies you with power to overcome that sin. Do not let a transgression go undealt with once it is found out, for thus shall you grow daily in grace.

There were three English ladies who served the Lord in the interior of China. One was engaged, while the other two vowed to remain single. Yet the sister who was engaged was the unhappiest of all. Although her fiancé wrote her often, which gave her comfort, she felt downcast soon afterwards. Spiritually speaking, she was one who drank but was thirsty again.

One day while she was in her room she felt terribly lonesome, so she cried again. The two other sisters then asked her why she felt lonesome. Was not her fiancé frequently writing to her? If anybody should feel lonesome, they observed, it should be *them*. After they had said these words, they returned to their room and began to feel lonesome too. They thought to themselves that they had every right to *be* lonesome since they were laboring for the Lord in the interior of China without good food and a good dwelling place! Alas, how sin is contagious!

Nevertheless, as they continued to be disturbed, they remembered the word of the Lord to His disciples: "I am with

you always, even unto the end of the world" (Matt. 28.20b). They
also recalled the word of the psalmist who said: "In thy presence
is fulness of joy; in thy right hand there are pleasures for ever-
more" (Ps. 16.11). Whereupon they knelt and prayed, "O Lord,
it is a sin to feel lonesome. You have said that You are with us
to the end of the world; therefore, we confess that feeling lonesome
is a sin. You have said that in Your presence is fulness of joy and
at Your right hand are pleasures forevermore; therefore, we
acknowledge that feeling lonesome is sin." And sure enough, once
they had dealt with this sin, loneliness never came back to them.
Hallelujah!

Each day we may discover a new sin or a new failure in our
lives, yet daily there can be the fresh supply of God's grace; "for
of his fulness we all received, and grace for grace" (John 1.16).
We shall receive, and receive again, of His grace.

One sister who was laboring for the Lord in India worried
a lot. One day she read Philippians 4.6: "In nothing be anxious;
but in everything by prayer and supplication with thanksgiving
let your requests be made known unto God." She saw that worry-
ing was sin and not giving thanks was also sin. Whenever we
realize what is sinful, let us come to the Lord and confess it; but
at the same time let us also confess that the Lord lives in us.
This will be growth in our lives.

The *nature* of victory in Christ is absolute and cannot be improved upon, but the *scope* of victory is ever enlarging. The light
each receives varies. One who receives more light makes more
progress, while the one who receives less light grows less. He who
knows more of what sin is receives more of God's supply, whereas
he who knows less of what sin is receives less supply from God.

We should understand the relationship of truth to us as well
as the relationship of grace to us. May we be before God daily,
saying, "O Lord, I cannot and I will not. I thank and praise You,
Lord, for I cannot." We should ask God daily to give us light
and grace. Even when we fail occasionally, we can immediately
be restored in a moment. If we walk day by day in such a

manner as this, who can tell how much we may grow? For all is done in and by Christ.

Hallelujah, this is perfect salvation! God will lead us to go forward in growth and advancement. Satan can do nothing. Praise the Lord, for Christ has already overcome!

9 | The Note of Victory

We will triumph in thy salvation, and in the name of our God we will set up our banners: Jehovah fulfil all thy petitions. (Ps. 20.5)

And it came to pass after this, that the children of Moab, and the children of Ammon, and with them some of the Ammonites, came against Jehoshaphat to battle. ... And Jehoshaphat feared, and set himself to seek unto Jehovah; and he proclaimed a fast throughout all Judah. ... O our God, wilt thou not judge them? for we have no might against this great company that cometh against us; neither know we what to do: but our eyes are upon thee. ... and he said, Hearken ye, all Judah, and ye inhabitants of Jerusalem, and thou king Jehoshaphat: Thus saith Jehovah unto you, Fear not ye, neither be dismayed by reason of this great multitude; for the battle is not yours, but God's. ... Ye shall not need to fight in this battle: set yourselves, stand ye still, and see the salvation of Jehovah with you, O Judah and Jerusalem; fear not, nor be dismayed: tomorrow go out against them; for Jehovah is with you. And Jehoshaphat bowed his head and his face to the ground; and all Judah and the inhabitants of Jerusalem fell down before Jehovah, worshipping Jehovah. And the Levites, of the children of the Kohathites and of the children of the Korahites, stood up to praise Jehovah, the God of Israel, with an exceeding loud voice. And they rose early in the morning and went forth into the wilderness of Tekoa: and as they went

forth, Jehoshaphat stood and said, Hear me, O Judah, and
ye inhabitants of Jerusalem: believe in Jehovah your God, so
shall ye be established; believe his prophets, so shall ye pros-
per. And when he had taken counsel with the people, he ap-
pointed them that should sing unto Jehovah, and give praise
in holy array, as they went out before the army, and say, Give
thanks unto Jehovah; for his lovingkindness endureth for ever.
And when they began to sing and to praise, Jehovah set liers-
in-wait against the children of Ammon, Moab, and mount Seir,
that were come against Judah; and they were smitten. . . . And
when Judah came to the watch-tower of the wilderness, they
looked upon the multitude; and, behold, they were dead bodies
fallen to the earth, and there were none that escaped. . . . And
on the fourth day they assembled themselves in the valley of
Beracah; for there they blessed Jehovah: therefore, the name
of that place was called The valley of Beracah unto this day.
Then they returned, every man of Judah and Jerusalem, and
Jehoshaphat in the forefront of them, to go again to Jerusalem
with joy; for Jehovah had made them to rejoice over their
enemies. And they came to Jerusalem with psalteries and harps
and trumpets unto the house of Jehovah. (2 Chron. 20.1, 3,
12, 15, 17–22, 24, 26–28)

In the past few messages, we have looked into this matter of
how a Christian can be victorious and continue to grow in grace.
We now need to look into another matter — the note of victory.
As we all know, sometimes people while singing may utter the
right words but do so with the wrong tune. The life that wins
has its own note and tune. In our lives of victory in Christ there
needs to be the right note as well as the right word.

In Psalm 20.5 the word "salvation" can also be translated as
"victory" (mg.), and the word "triumph" can be translated as "rejoice." Accordingly, this verse may read as either "We will rejoice
in thy salvation" or "We will triumph in thy victory." Actually,

there is no difference between salvation and victory, because they are the two phases of one thing.

Perhaps you do not understand what I mean by the *note* of victory. Let me put it another way by saying that victory has its hallmark. How do you know you have victory? When do you know you have victory? The answer is what Psalm 20.5 tells us: "We will *triumph* in thy victory."

Victory and Triumphing in Victory are Different

Do we know the difference between victory and triumphing in victory? The first is that which is totally done by Christ, whereas the second is that which is done by us. Victory is the work of Christ, but triumphing in victory is our work. Victory is that work which prevails; triumphing in victory is the boasting after victory is secured. For instance, in my earlier days I often played cricket. Admittedly, the ball was heavy and the hands ached after playing a while. In a match that would last an hour, we play and sweat, hitting the ball through one wicket after another until hopefully we win. Whenever our school team did win, our fellow students would wave their hats and handkerchiefs and shout for joy. And this could be called a triumphing in victory. The school *team* had won the victory, but our *fellow students* in the school triumphed in the victory. Similarly, in the spiritual realm, we can thank God that the victory is all accomplished by Christ! We have not shed any blood at all; nevertheless, *we* can triumph in victory.

Every Christian will triumph in victory once he obtains the victory of Christ. If there is no hallelujah but only a fountain of tears, then there can be no triumph in victory. Ours is a joyful note because of the salvation of the Lord. We triumph in His victory. When we won the cricket match, we gave the school the victory so that our fellow students could triumph in it. Likewise, our Lord himself has overcome; and He has given that victory to us to let us triumph in it.

Let us shout, Hallelujah! Christ is Victor! I will not say that he who cannot say Hallelujah has not overcome, but I *will* say that he does not have the right note of victory. The *tone* of victory is very important. For if the tone or sound is not right, people will doubt your victory, and you probably will wonder too. Peter's accent was Galilean; even a maid could distinguish it. Do we lack that Galilean accent? Or will our voice manifest our victory? May we daily have the Galilean accent so that people recognize that we have followed Jesus the Galilean.

The Triumph of Jehoshaphat

In the Old Testament period, Judah had a king named Jehoshaphat. Let us listen to his note of victory as the story is unfolded for us in 2 Chronicles 20.

"The children of Moab, and the children of Ammon, and with them some of the Ammonites, came against Jehoshaphat to battle" (v.1). At that time, the nation of Judah was very weak. She was helpless against the invading foes. As Jehoshaphat looked at himself, he naturally was full of fear. He was helpless now as he was helpless before. These same old enemies came again. What could he do about them? He was totally helpless.

Nonetheless he feared God. Hence he "set himself to seek unto Jehovah; and he proclaimed a fast throughout all Judah" (v.3). He had no other recourse but to come before God.

He prayed, saying, "O our God, wilt thou not judge them? for we have no might against this great company that cometh against us; neither know we what to do: but our eyes are upon thee" (v.12). He confessed that they had no might of their own, but their eyes were upon God. Let us pause here to make an observation. We have been emphasizing throughout this series of messages that the conditions for yielding are: first, I cannot; and second, I will not; but that as a consequence, we must believe God. This was precisely what Jehoshaphat did. He confessed that they had no strength to fight against the enemies and that they did not know what to do. Yet he prayed, "O God, our eyes are upon thee."

God immediately sent a prophet to them and said, "Fear not ye, neither be dismayed by reason of this great multitude; for the battle is not yours, but God's" (v.15b). The battle is the Lord's. Whether victory or defeat, it has nothing to do with you. Ill-temper, pride, doubt, unclean thoughts, greediness, and all sorts of other sins have no relationship to you—because the battle is not yours, it is God's. Jehovah said, "Ye shall not need to fight in this battle: set yourselves, stand ye still" (v.17a). God wants you to stand still. He wants you to let go completely. You only need to stand there "and see the salvation of Jehovah with you" (v.17b). Do recognize this fact clearly that you and I are not combatants, we are observers. Whenever we do not triumph in victory, we are defeated. Let us not be afraid, because God fights for us.

Jehoshaphat took a further step. He not only stood still and watched by the side, he bowed his head with his face to the ground and worshiped God. All Judah and the inhabitants of Jerusalem likewise fell before God and worshiped. As he and Judah were attacked by such a great multitude, what did he do? He called the Levites to stand up to praise the Lord. He caused them to go before the army and praise Jehovah in holy array. Was he mad in so doing? The people of the Levites feared neither stones nor arrows. They sang praises to the Lord. And this is the note of victory. This note comes after you know that *the Lord* has given you the victory and that you have overcome your enemy. Men will counsel that when you see temptation coming, you are to strive and resist. But God makes clear that "when they began to sing and to praise, Jehovah set liers-in-wait against the children of Ammon, Moab, and Mount Seir, that were come against Judah; and they were smitten" (v.22). Whenever there is singing and praising of the Lord, there the enemy is defeated.

What was the result? "When Judah came to the watch-tower of the wilderness, they looked upon the multitude; and, behold,

The Life That Wins

they were dead bodies fallen to the earth, and there were none
that escaped" (v.24). When God gives victory, He will not let any
escape. We probably would leave five or six untouched, but the
Lord will not allow any enemy to slip through. It is very mean-
ingful that when they began to sing and to praise, the Lord sent
liers-in-wait to smite the children of Ammon, Moab and Mount
Seir who came to attack Judah. God can only work when you
begin praising. Whenever you praise, He works.

I know you have many trials and temptations. These may
be in the form of a physical weakness, an adverse circumstance
or a business crisis. You will say, what can I do? How can I overcome? You may know victory, but by the very asking of these
questions it is plain that your note is not right. When you see
temptation or trial or trouble coming, you should instead say,
Hallelujah! As you say Hallelujah, the enemy is defeated. For
our God will work only when you begin to praise. He works the
moment you sing.

It is not enough that you confess your inability and believe
in God's ability. You should sing from your heart a Hallelujah!
You should say, God, I thank You because I am tempted and
I am helpless. I thank You, for Your victory is mine. Observe
Jehoshaphat, who sang because he believed he had the victory.
In the eyes of Jehoshaphat, all his enemies were dead bodies.
So he advanced and continued singing. He was not afraid of
stones and arrows, for he reckoned his enemies as dead. And
as the children of Israel looked out of the watchtower, they in-
deed saw the dead bodies of their enemies.

Two Stages of Thanksgiving and Praise

"And on the fourth day they assembled themselves in the valley
of Beracah; for there they blessed Jehovah: . . . Then they returned, every man of Judah and Jerusalem, and Jehoshaphat
in the forefront of them, to go again to Jerusalem with joy; for
Jehovah had made them to rejoice over their enemies. And they

came to Jerusalem with psalteries and harps and trumpets unto the house of Jehovah" (vv.26a, 27–28). Thanks and praise are in two stages: the first stage is before accomplishment, the other one is after accomplishment. The great error today is not to praise *before* accomplishment, to hold back praise until it can be seen what will happen. Many brothers and sisters have confessed their inability and have given up the thought of trying to be able. They have also believed in God's fact that Christ is their victory. But they dare not say, Hallelujah, I have overcome! As one brother admitted, "I want to see if it works." Or as a sister said, "I want to see if it is effective." What they meant was that they would only commence to praise God if this proved to be working or effective tomorrow. Yet Jehoshaphat praised *twice*. Every overcomer has this *double* praise. Praise *before* the physical eyes see, and praise *after* the eyes have seen. And this is the sound of victory, this is the note of triumph. But when there is no praise, the battle is lost.

You ask whether there is victory, and I ask whether there is a Hallelujah. For Hallelujah is the note of victory. The *right* note expresses *genuine* victory. It is something beyond pretension. All who overcome sound a certain note. They are joyous and they always praise. By distinguishing a person's accent, you know where that one comes from geographically. Similarly, by listening to the note of a Christian, you know whether he has overcome. The mark of spiritual victory is the ability to say Hallelujah, the ability to say, Praise the Lord, when temptation comes. If you continually look at yourself you are unable to praise. But if you see Christ, immediately you can fill the air with a Hallelujah, praise the Lord! It does not matter if the temptation is stronger, or if the children of Moab and Ammon are more numerous, since the battle is the Lord's and not ours. The Lord is fully responsible for all.

Hence the note of victory is joyous thanks and praise to God. You need not wait till you are actually defeated, defiled and have sinned seriously before you acknowledge your defeat. No, whenever you lose the note of thanks and praise, you have already lost the victory. You need not sin grossly; as long as you are unable to triumph in victory—that is to say, unable to be joyful and to praise and thank God—you have been defeated. Let us clearly understand that the victorious life which God has given us may joyfully sing Hallelujah every day. When the note of praise is missing, the victory is lost.

Keep Victory in Joy

There is a familiar verse in the Bible, which is Nehemiah 8.10c: "the joy of Jehovah is your strength." How does the life which God has given us express itself? Through joy. The very air which our Lord Jesus Christ breathed was full of joy and praise. I am still learning this lesson in these years. I have been forgiven, I have consecrated myself, and I have been obedient; yet I feel somewhat miserable, and I murmur a little. I cannot say from the heart, Thanks and praise be to the Lord.

Whenever we cannot say, Praise the Lord, we are already defeated. Oh! Let us all realize that our victory is in the joy of the Lord. Whenever we lose that joy, we immediately lose the victory. We become deflated when that joy is gone. Hence we must keep our victory in the strength of joy. One brother said that he had never known the strength of joy until these days. Victory must be kept in the joy of the Lord as fish must be kept in water.

Rejoice in Afflictions

Yet how *can* we be joyful? We can quite easily and naturally be joyful and praise God in those things that are pleasant—such as when we cross the threshold of victory or of power. But the Scriptures tell us to be joyful even in many unpleasant things.

"How that in much proof of affliction the abundance of their joy . . . abounded . . ." (2 Cor. 8.2). Here we are told that the

Macedonian believers had abundant joy in time of great affliction. What they had was not merely a drop or two of joy, but
joy in abundance. Let us always rejoice with abundant joy, even
in great affliction. The life of Christ is the life that wins; therefore,
we can triumph in victory. We can praise God with joy even when
a great army is attacking us. The characteristic of victory is to
be filled with thanksgiving and praise in time of affliction.

Once a brother was a railroad switchman. One day he was
hit by a train and lost one of his legs. When he woke up in the
hospital, he was asked if he could still thank and praise the Lord.
He answered that he praised and thanked God that only *one* leg
was cut off! Oh, what a positive difference there is in this brother!
For this is the note of victory, a sound of thanks and praise in
the midst of great affliction.

"Count it all joy, my brethren, when ye fall into manifold
trials" (James 1.2 mg.). "Wherein ye greatly rejoice, though now
for a little while, if need be, ye have been put to grief in manifold
trials" (1 Peter 1.6). "Whom not having seen ye love; on whom,
though now ye see him not, yet believing, ye rejoice greatly with
joy unspeakable and full of glory" (1 Peter 1.8). "Beloved, think
it not strange concerning the fiery trial among you, which cometh upon you to prove you, as though a strange thing happened
unto you: but insomuch as ye are partakers of Christ's sufferings, rejoice; that at the revelation of his glory also ye may rejoice with exceeding joy" (1 Peter 4.12–13).

These verses show us how to live in the midst of trial. James
tells us of manifold temptations, whether expected or unexpected,
coming from foes or from friends, from the heathen or from the
brethren, with good reason or not. All kinds of trial will come,
yet none should cause us to lose our joy. Remember that when
the Bible mentions joy, it often uses such descriptions as "greatly
rejoice" or "exceeding joy" or "all joy" or "joy unspeakable." For
what God gives is always exceedingly great and full. The joy
spoken of in 1 Peter 1.6 is "greatly rejoice"; whereas the "grief"
mentioned is "for a little while." Is grief permitted? Grief seems

to be unavoidable. Having eyes, tears will fall. Although tears are falling, there is still joy. Hence in 1.8 of 1 Peter, the word of God observes this: "yet believing, ye rejoice greatly with joy unspeakable and full of glory." This joy is unspeakable. How many times before the tears have dried up, the mouth has already uttered, Hallelujah! Or while the tears are still falling, the mouth has said, Thank and praise the Lord!

Many people shed tears on the one hand, yet praise and thank God on the other. Do recall the words of the hymn, "If the Path I Travel," written by sister Margaret E. Barber:* "Let the spirit praise Thee, though the heart be riven." While living on earth, your heart cannot help but be riven sometimes, for it has its feeling; yet your spirit is still joyful. According to the word of 1 Peter 4.12, you rejoice not only *during* the time of trial but you also rejoice when the trial initially "cometh upon you." In other words, you *welcome* trial. You thank and praise the Lord for trial is coming.

Some brothers and sisters "lock their eyebrows" when they see trial approaching. But Peter says to rejoice and thank the Lord for its coming. For whenever you are able to thank and praise Him, you are above the trial. There is nothing that enables us to rise above temptation, environment and trouble more than joy and thanks and praise. This is the note of victory which an overcomer ought to sound.

In Chefoo, one sister who had only recently crossed the threshold of victory was severely tested. Her daughter died a few hours later while her husband was far away from home. Many brothers and sisters went to comfort her. Though her eyes were flooded with tears, her face showed smiles. She testified that the loss of a child was indeed painful, yet she could not understand why she was joyful. She thanked and praised God. Those brothers and sisters who went to comfort her were comforted by her in

---

*Miss Barber was a missionary lady from England, who was a great help to Watchman Nee's spiritual life.—*Translator*

stead. This is something no one can pretend. Victory is to be
kept by such a note as this. Even in trial there is praise and thanks
ascending to God.

Today we Christians on earth are to be God's examples. Are
these examples of ours beautiful? Are we different from the world?
If we cry as the world cries and laugh as the world laughs, where
is our victory? And where is God's victory? We ought to let the
world see that we have joy and strength. Though the world may
look at us as mad, yet they cannot help admiring the Christ who
causes us to appear as though mad. May God be gracious to
us that we may manifest the victory of Christ in afflictions.

"Blessed are ye when men shall reproach you, and persecute
you, and say all manner of evil against you falsely, for my sake.
Rejoice and be exceedingly glad: for great is your reward in
heaven: for so persecuted they the prophets that were before you"
(Matt. 5.11–12). When men reproach you, you may say you will
be patient. When men revile you, you may say you will not speak
back. Do not think that being patient and not speaking back are
enough. The fact of the matter is you are already defeated. For
to endure and not speak back is something the *world* is able to
do. The Buddhists and the Confucianists can do *that*. You ought
to be different from them. When men reproach you, you ought
to be able to say in the victory of Christ, "Lord, I thank and
praise You," for you consider men's reproach as something joyful.
When men persecute you, you ought to say in the triumph of
Christ, "Lord, I thank and praise You," because you take their
persecution as something to be joyous about. If yours is a genuine victory, you will rejoice and be exceedingly glad. A so-called
victory that only endures what the world can endure is not genuine victory, but suppression. What the Lord does is always that
which brings joy.

In the light of all that has been said, then, the issue here is
whether or not the note is right. Today's problem lies in con-
sidering silent patience as virtue par excellence. But when you
are reproached by men, are you able to be exceedingly glad? Or

do you merely look downward and keep quiet? Many are being persecuted. Many sisters are persecuted by their husbands. Many are being falsely and evilly spoken against. What, sisters, do you do? Do you ask the Lord to keep you from losing your temper so that you will not explode? Do you consider not exploding to be victory? You may think you have overcome, but this is not a victory which is given by the Lord. Were it *His* victory, you would be able to praise and thank Him greatly in the midst of man's reproach and persecution. Let me reiterate that whenever you do not thank and praise God, you are already defeated. For the note and sound of victory is thanks and praise.

Once a brother in the Lord found himself sitting next to his great enemy in a tramcar. He asked the Lord to preserve him. Outwardly he maintained a good attitude by talking to his foe, even talking with him about the current news concerning an upcoming athletic event. But inwardly he was telling the Lord to hasten that foe's departure from the car so that he might maintain his victory. He sighed after arriving at his destination and said it was not easy to have gained this victory. Yet was this a genuine victory in the Lord? Permit me to speak frankly that this was but a lying victory, a man-made victory, an empty triumph. Had it been God's victory, he would not have needed to ask the Lord to keep him and give him patience; rather, he would have said to God that he thanked and praised Him for putting him in such a situation. Even if the ride were longer, it would not matter to him at all.

"Rejoice in the Lord always" (Phil. 4.4a). Whenever the word of God mentions joy, it is often either couched in terms of "exceeding joy" or "full of joy" or "rejoice always." "Always" here means persistently. Have you heard it? If you have not heard, then "again I will say, Rejoice" (4.4b). Such is the thrust of what Paul means to say: if it has not registered with you the first time I said it, then I will say again to you to rejoice! The life that God gives is a joyous one. Joy is the daily expression of a Christian's walk. In spite of tribulation and trials, there is still joy. Its opposite is anxiety. Many are anxious about their children, money or business. But the word of the Lord declares: "In *nothing* be anxious" (Phil. 4.6). We think we have reason to be anxious, but the Lord counters with, "In nothing be anxious," so that we may always rejoice.

We sin if we are not joyful even for a single day. Once at a meeting a brother spoke on the theme "In Nothing Be Anxious." One sister present was very unhappy when she heard the message. She argued, how could anyone *not* be anxious! If the brothers were more anxious, she observed, the sisters might eat better food (this she said because the brothers were in charge of meals that day). The Lord, however, would not let her go till she saw that anxiety was sin indeed. Finally, she obtained the victory.

"Wherefore I take pleasure in weaknesses, in injuries, in necessities, in persecutions, in distresses, for Christ's sake: for when I am weak, then am I strong" (2 Cor. 12.10). Paul took weaknesses, injuries, necessities, persecutions and distresses as pleasure and joy. None of you knows what will happen to you. You realize your path on earth will not be entirely smooth. Some of you may have sick relatives, some may face the death of loved ones, and others may encounter persecution. What will you do? If you tell the Lord that you will be patient, your very word will prove to be your defeat. But if you say, "Lord, I thank and praise You," you shall prevail. For then Christ will be manifested in you. Because you give the Lord opportunity to show forth His power, therefore, you can afford to be joyful. Such ought to be your daily life on earth. May you rejoice in the Lord always and offer thanks and praise to His Name.

"In everything give thanks" (1 Thess. 5.18a). "And whatsoever ye do, in word or in deed, do all in the name of the Lord Jesus, giving thanks to God the Father through him" (Col. 3.17). These two verses are all-inclusive. Let us thank and praise God, and let us say Hallelujah. The world of men may be perplexed at our attitude; nonetheless, we still give thanks in all things. And if this is in fact our manner, no temptation or trial can ever be our match. Nothing can touch us. We have the faith to meet temptation, and we can thank and praise God in trial, because we are obedient to Him.

Some may misunderstand my words here as meaning that I oppose patience. By way of clarification I wish to say that patience is something most precious. We *do* need to have patience, but not the kind that is derived from clenching one's teeth! "Unto all patience and longsuffering with joy" (Cor. 1.11). Patience with joy, not forced patience out of reluctance or sorrow. No, the note of a Christian's daily life is "unto all patience and longsuffering *with joy.*" "In *everything* give thanks"— such is life in the third heaven.

"More than Conquerors"

Why is it that life is not to be considered victorious unless there is joy? Why do we need to be joyous in order to prove and demonstrate this life that wins? "In all these things we are more than conquerors" (Rom. 8.37). The victory which *God* bestows on us is of one kind only, which is to say, that "in *all* these things we more than conquer" (Darby). To barely conquer is not the kind of victory which the Lord bestows. What He gives us is always that "we more than conquer." To barely conquer is no victory at all. But if it be "more than conquer," then there is a joy that pervades it all and proves that this is a victory from God.

Let us realize that what we have is a cup that is running over. Whatever the Lord gives, it always runs over every natural limitation or boundary. If it does not do so, it is not given by Him. The victory the Lord grants is of such magnitude that "whosoever smiteth thee on thy right cheek, turn to him the other also. And if any man would go to law with thee, and take away thy coat, let him have thy cloak also. And whosoever shall compel thee to go one mile, go with him two" (Matt. 5.39b-41). A victory with *leftovers* is truly God's victory. To *barely* overcome is the result of men's own work.

This, then, is the genuine note of victory. May God open our eyes to perceive that unless our victory is one in which "we more than conquer," it is only an imitation — it is merely suppression. But if Christ truly lives in us, we will be able to be joyous and thankful in *all* circumstances. We will be able to say "Hallelujah, praise God!" from now even to eternity.

10 | Consecration

The love of Christ constraineth us; because we thus judge, that one died for all, therefore all died; and he died for all, that they that live should no longer live unto themselves, but unto him who for their sakes died and rose again. (2 Cor. 5.14-15).

Neither present your members unto sin as instruments of unrighteousness; but present yourselves unto God, as alive from the dead, and your members as instruments of righteousness unto God. (Rom. 6.13)

Know ye not, that to whom ye present yourselves as servants unto obedience, his servants ye are whom ye obey; whether of sin unto death, or of obedience unto righteousness? (Rom. 6.16)

I beseech you therefore, brethren, to present your bodies a living sacrifice, holy, acceptable to God, which is your spiritual service. And be not fashioned according to this world: but be ye transformed by the renewing of your mind, that ye may prove what is the good and acceptable and perfect will of God. (Rom. 12.1-2)

I speak after the manner of men because of the infirmity of your flesh: for as ye presented your members as servants unto uncleanness and to iniquity unto iniquity, even so now present your members as servants to righteousness unto sanctification. (Rom. 6.19)

Being made free from sin and become servants to God,

ye have your fruit unto sanctification, and the end eternal life.
(Rom. 6.22)

Before we conclude this series of messages on the life that
wins, it is imperative that we discuss one more subject — that of
consecration. For without this, our life of victory will not reach
its summit.

Consecration is actually the first thing one does after receiving the life that wins. It is that which one should do after he
is saved. On the one hand, there are many who have been saved
but have never consecrated themselves. This makes consecration
absolutely necessary upon their entering into victory. On the other
hand, there are some people who, though they consecrated
themselves to the Lord when they were first saved, have for many
years led a life of continual ups and downs. What they need to
do is to consecrate themselves afresh. I dare not say that for others
consecration is to be the first act or first expression after victory.
I can only say that since the Lord died and rose again for *me*,
the first thing I myself would do after entering victory would
be to consecrate myself.

Some contend that consecration must be done *before* victory.
Consecrate, and then conquer. But Romans 6.13 would indicate
otherwise: "Neither present your members unto sin as instruments
of unrighteousness; but *present yourselves unto God, as alive from the
dead*, and your members as instruments of righteousness unto
God"— thereby indicating consecration *after* victory. One thing
is clear however: without death and resurrection, one cannot
possibly present himself to God. Only a person who has died
and risen can offer himself as a living sacrifice. We have talked
previously about co-crucifixion with Christ and about the Lord
living in us. We have died and now live with the Lord. In accor-
dance with Romans 6.13, a Christian consecrates himself after
he has received the life that wins. Without such life, one's con-

secration will be rejected by God. For He does not want anything that belongs to Adam and death.

Without this life that wins, a person's consecration is undependable. One day consecrated, but the next day forgotten: today a vow made before God that one is willing to do this or that for Him; tomorrow the vow forgotten. One missionary had attended the Keswick Convention held in England seven times. She confessed that each year she attended Keswick it was like having a watch spring rewound. Annually she had to be reset. Numerous Christians are like this sister. They promise God much in a convention or conference, only to forget all about it afterwards. This proves that we do not have the strength to consecrate.

Without the life that wins, your consecration will not be accepted by God. Because what you offer belongs to Adam, and it is dead. Only that which comes from the Lord may be presented to God. What comes out of self is unfit to be offered.

Let us therefore know that the first act after having the life that wins ought to be a consecration of ourselves to God. Now is the time and opportunity to offer; otherwise, there will be a drawing back after a few days.

The Basis and Motive of Consecration

Both Romans 6 and Romans 12 speak of consecration. Why do we present our bodies as living sacrifices? Paul beseeches us by the mercies of God. What are the mercies of God? Romans 1–8 describe His mercies. According to the accepted understanding of the book of Romans on this subject of consecration, Romans 12 follows in thought the first eight chapters (with Romans 9–11 serving as a lengthy parenthesis in which Paul directs his attention towards the Jews and salvation). The things described in the first eight chapters are God's mercies. In the past we were sinners, but God's Son came to earth to atone for our sins through the shedding of His blood. Chapters 3 and 4 speak of the blood and faith; chapter 5, of forgiveness and justification; chapters 6-8, of the cross. On the one hand, the blood is for the remission of sins so that we may receive forgiveness; on the other hand, the cross is for the death of our old man that we may be delivered from the power of sin. Thank God, Christ died on the cross for us, and He also lives for us. And on the basis of such mercies of God, the Holy Spirit through Paul begs us to present ourselves to God.

We ought to know the purpose of God in creating us and in redeeming us. He wishes for us to manifest the life of His Son and share in His Son's glory. Even before the foundation of the world, God has purposed one purpose, which is to say, that He wants to have many sons just as He has the Only Begotten Son. And thus it states in Romans 8.29: "whom he foreknew, he also foreordained to be conformed to the image of his Son, that he might be the firstborn *among many brethren.*" Why has God done such things? Because He had foreordained us to be conformed to the image of His Son. This is the eternal purpose of God. He purchases and redeems us that He may possess us.

Yet God uses two means to possess us: one is on His side, the other is on our side. *On His side,* God sent His Son to die for us, to buy us back. According to the right of purchase, we are His bondslaves. Thank the Lord, He has bought us. God once said to Abraham, "He that is born in the house, and he that is bought with money, must needs be circumcised" (Gen. 17.13). Hallelujah, we are not only born of God we are also bought by Him.

We are bought by God and thus belong to Him, yet He sets us free. Although according to the right of redemption, we belong to God, He nonetheless will not force us into service. He will let us go if we desire to serve mammon, the world, the belly, or other idols. For the moment God is inactive: He is waiting for us to move: till one day we say *on our side:* "O God, I am Your bondslave not only because You have bought me, but also because I will gladly serve You." A verse in Romans 6 unveils a most precious principle concerning consecration. We become God's bondslaves not only for the reason that He has bought us, but also for the reason "that to whom ye present yourselves as servants unto obedience, his servants ye are whom ye obey" (v.16a).

Here, then, are the two means by which God possesses us. On the one side, we are His bondslaves because He has bought us; on the other side, we willingly and gladly present ourselves to Him as His bondslaves. As regards law, we become God's bondslaves on the day He purchased and redeemed us. As regards experience, we become His bondslaves on the day we offer up ourselves to Him. From the viewpoint of right and ownership, we are God's bondslaves on the day we were redeemed. From the viewpoint of practice, we are truly His bondslaves on the day when we voluntarily and gladly give ourselves over to Him.

Consequently, no one will ever be ignorant about his being a bondslave of God, for in order to be His bondslave, the believer will always need to voluntarily present himself. Such consecration is totally one's own choice and initiative. Hence the offerer will know what he is doing. God will not coerce a person to serve Him. And that is why Paul, knowing the heart of God, does not force, he only "beseeches" (see Rom. 12.1a). God delights to see His people offer themselves willingly to Him.

The victorious life and salvation are intimately related. At the time we were saved, we quite naturally would want to present ourselves, because the new life in us has constrained us to do so. Every saved person knows he ought to live for the Lord. Nevertheless, we have no strength. We are surrounded by many contrary things and are not able to live for the Lord. Thank God, though, He gives Christ to us, thus enabling us to consecrate ourselves to Him. We could not be a living sacrifice when we were dead in sins. We were still unable even after we were saved if we continued to live in sins. But now that we have crossed the threshold of victory, Christ is our life and our holiness; consequently, we are able to offer ourselves to God willingly and joyfully.

Mr. D. M. Panton told the story of an African slave girl about to be auctioned. Two men bid against each other to purchase her. Both of these men were wicked. The slave girl knew her life would be miserable if she fell into the hands of either. So she wept much. Suddenly a third man joined the bidding. The price continued to rise till the first two men could not afford to bid anymore. And thus the girl was bought by the third man. He immediately called a blacksmith to break the girl's chains. He then announced her freedom by saying, "I bought you not to make you my slave; I bought you to make you free." Having said that, he walked away. The girl was perplexed for two minutes. She "woke up" and chased after the man, declaring that from now on till she died she would be his slave.

Now the love of this man towards the slave girl is much like the love Christ has towards us. And as we are constrained by this love, we too will tell the Lord that henceforth we are His willing slaves. God has bought us and He has brought us through death and resurrection. We have received His manifold mercies and therefore we ought to present ourselves freely to God as living sacrifices.

Romans 6 speaks of presenting our*selves*—especially our *members*—to God; whereas Romans 12 speaks of presenting our *bodies* as living sacrifices. So much is included in this latter consecration. In our previous discussions we talked about letting go and believing so that we might live out the life of God and fulfill His demand. God's demand is none other than that we wholly consecrate ourselves to Him. Such demand is all-inclusive. This is something we cannot do by ourselves; only through the indwelling Christ may we respond to this demand. Naturally speaking, we cannot; but now through Christ we can. Because we have received mercies, we are able.

It was the custom in Old Testament times for a Hebrew slave to serve his master for six years. In the seventh year, he might go out free. If he said he loved his master and would not go out free, his master would bring him to the judge and then to the door to have his ear bored through with an awl. And thus would he serve his master forever (see Ex. 21.2-6). God has saved us and bought us with His blood. He has not redeemed us with corruptible things such as silver and gold, but with the precious blood of His own Son. Initially many Christians feel obliged to serve God for the sake of conscience, until one day they truly know the loveliness of Christ and cannot help but present themselves to the Lord willingly and gladly. And as they so offer themselves, the Lord will bring them to the door and pierce through their ear with an awl. The doorpost is where the blood was customarily applied at the time of Passover. Today they too have shed their blood, for they have been brought to the cross. They love the Lord, and therefore they want to be His slave forever. Because He loves them, they will serve Him forever. Now if you are like these Christians, you cannot help but say, "O Lord, You loved me, saved me and liberated me. I love You, I must serve You forever."

Things to Present

1. Persons—The first item to be presented is our loved ones. If you do not love the Lord more than parents, wife, children and friends, you cannot be Christ's disciple. But if you offer all to the Lord, no one else will occupy and control your heart anymore as long as you live. The reason why God saves you is to wholly possess you. Many tears, many human affections and many sorrowful hearts will try to pull you back. Nevertheless, you must say, "O Lord, all my relationships with people I have placed on the altar. I have been detached from all of them."

Paul Rader's wife was sick. People asked this minister of God in America why he did not pray for his wife. He answered that the Lord had not yet asked him to pray for her. Another brother asked him if he would not feel terribly sad if his wife should depart from the world. He replied that she had already departed (since brother Rader had previously offered his wife on the altar of consecration)!

God wanted a servant of the Lord to lay down his best friend. And his response to God was this: "I am willing if You so desire."

God gives us the life that wins that we may obey His will as well as know His will. Never think that the victorious life is only, negatively, not sinning. It as well, positively speaking, enables us to commune with God and obey His will. God gives us this life not for the sake of fulfilling our purpose but for us to fulfill His. Therefore, no Christian should clasp a handhold on any other person. Without presenting all persons and friendships in our lives, we cannot satisfy God's heart. Persons must go. We need to be able to say from the heart: "Whom have I in heaven but thee? And there is none upon earth that I desire besides thee" (Ps. 73.25). We also need to say, "I will love the Lord my God with all my heart, with all my soul, and with all my mind" (see Matt. 22.37).

I have so appreciated our sister Margaret E. Barber.* She was truly one who loved the Lord with all her heart, soul and mind. After her death, the following words were found written in her Bible after Matthew 22.37 ("Thou shalt love the Lord thy God with all thy heart, and with all thy soul, and with all thy mind"): "O Lord, I thank You, because You have such a command." How often we are distressed by having to notice the many commands of God. We should instead say what sister Barber wrote: "O Lord, I thank You, because You have such a command."

In this matter of consecration, God will not allow you to hold on to even that which He himself has *given* you. He will not allow you to hold on to your father and mother, your wife and children and friends. Even the Isaac born to *promise* needs to be laid on the altar. The failure of many Christians today is due to their being entangled by people.

---

*See footnote in previous chapter on Miss Barber.—*Translator*

2. Affairs—Not just persons but many affairs should be offered up to God as well. How many are the affairs which we decide to do without seeking the will of God. One brother resolved that he must graduate first in his class and also rank first in his college entrance examination. As a result, he spent all his time and energy on education. After he knew victory, however, he laid this matter in God's hand and was freely resigned to whatever His will might be.

Although it may be good to spend a great deal of your time on your business, it will not be profitable to you if your intimate communion with God suffers as a consequence. If for your business you have a certain expectation which you will not give up, then you will feel you simply must obtain your goal. In that case you need to consecrate your business. You must not be brought under the power of anything.

Many brothers hope to get ahead of other people through education. This is their proud anticipation. I do not say they should quit school; I only say they must be willing to lay down everything if the Lord should call them. A true story can perhaps help to illustrate what has just been said. A Christian brother was an orphan, and his family situation was very poor. He had good penmanship as well as an excellent musical talent. In the orphanage, others learned carpentry and masonry, but he was able to attend high school because he obtained a scholarship every term. When he finished two years of college education, the school administration intended to send him on to St. John's University (in Shanghai) for another two years before sending him to America for further study. The condition was that he must serve in his alma mater upon his return from abroad. Both his mother and his uncle wrote to congratulate him.

Now at this point he was still not a Christian. But just two months ago this young man was saved, and at the same time he consecrated his life to God. One day during this period since his conversion, I asked him what his final decision would be with respect to his future education. He replied that he had decided

to accept the school's offer. Actually, he was on the verge of sign-
ing the agreement. He even said to me that I ought to know and
appreciate his ambition after being a schoolmate of his for eight
years.

When we parted, I said to him, "Today we are brothers; but
when you return from the States, I wonder if you will still be
my brother." Upon hearing this, he went to the Lord and prayed,
"O God, You know my ambition; yet You have called me. I by
myself cannot lay down my ambition. Lord, if You will, I am
willing even to go to the rural areas and preach the gospel."

After he finished praying, he went to the school principal and
told him he would not sign the agreement since he was not going on to university. His principal thought he must be mad. But
he said that the Lord had called him to preach the gospel.

Four days later, his uncle, cousins and mother all came to
see him. His mother wept, saying, "All these years since your
father died, I have worked hard with the hope that one day you
would be able to forge ahead. Today you have the opportunity
to advance, but now you refuse." His mother cried and cried.
His uncle too said this: "Before you entered the orphanage, I
took care of you. I even took care of your mother. Now you must
take responsibility over these two families. Your cousins here do
not have the money to go to school; but you have received such
a splendid opportunity, and yet you are now intent on throwing
it into the water." They even came to me and said: "Mr. Nee,
your parents do not need your support, but we need him to support our living."

Our brother was truly at a critical crossroads. So he asked
the Lord what he should do. He eventually saw that he owed
the Lord far more than he owed to men. And as a result he obeyed
God. Later, he did fulfill his responsibility to his mother and
uncle by supplying their necessities, although he could never yield
to their earlier expectation of him.

All of us should present our service to God. I do not say that
all should go out to preach, but I do say we all must offer

everything to God. Today's error lies in misunderstanding consecration as preaching, although we consecrate ourselves to do God's will. Many upon truly consecrating themselves discover that the Lord, far from wanting them to be ministers of the gospel, wants them to work hard in business in order that they may support the work of God being done by others.

3. *Things* — Not only persons and affairs, but many *things* also need to be consecrated to the Lord. With some, it may be ornaments; with others, it may be property; with still others, clothing. What needs to be consecrated may not be much, but you must not allow something little to remain as a hindrance in your life. In consecration, perhaps gold ornaments or fashionable dresses or money itself must be taken away from you. Yet this is not to be taken as a law.

Many waste their money; and this is unacceptable to God. Many lay up their wealth; yet this is equally displeasing to God Wasting has no place before the Lord; but neither does laying up for oneself have any place before Him. We need not use up all money at once; yet we must transfer it all to God's account. There is no such teaching of the tithe in the New Testament, since all must be placed in God's hand. The day you bring any money home, you should pray: "O God, all this money is yours. Out of it *You* give *me* my household expenses and not that *I* will give *You* the *leftovers* after I have used it." I dare not say that God will necessarily take all from you. Yet after you really offer to Him, all of it is His nonetheless.

I am ashamed to say it, but there are many brothers and sisters who do not look like God's people because of some decoration in their house, some clothing they wear, or some property they hold. If God touches you and deals with you concerning these things, you should offer them up to Him. Many aged saints need to be careful in writing their wills. What they write therein will frequently reveal what kind of Christian they *really* are. God has taken you and your property out of the world; you should not let it return to the world. When the children of Israel came out of Egypt, not a hoof was left behind. We should therefore not leave a single hoof in the world. In and of ourselves we are not able to do such a thing; we are weak; but thank God, all things are possible through Him. For does not His word say that "I can do all things in him that strengtheneth me"? (Phil. 4.13) This means that when I am empowered by the *Lord*, I *can* do all things — even let go of valuable material blessings. Though by ourselves we are unable to offer all, yet through the One who empowers us, we are well able to do so. For *Christ* is now our life; therefore, we are able.

Many young brothers and sisters give offerings to the Lord when they have only a little money. But when their money increases, they give even less than before. If the Lord has our heart, He should also have our pocketbook. The heart is important; but so is money. Unless the pocketbook is opened, the heart will never be opened.

4. Self—Not only persons, affairs and things need to be consecrated; the very last thing to be consecrated is your very own self. You should offer yourself to God to do His will. I do not know what your future holds, but I do know this one thing: that God has a definite purpose for each one of us. It may not be in the way of prosperity, nor may it necessarily be in the way of suffering. Yet regardless whether it be blessing or suffering, you must be willing to offer yourself to God's will. Many who are willing to be used by the Lord are filled with the Holy Spirit and live a victorious life because they have consecrated themselves to God.

What is to be presented? We are to present our bodies as living sacrifices. The Scriptures never once tell us to present our hearts; it tells us to present our bodies. For no one who has presented himself to God leaves his body unpresented. We present our whole being to the Lord. From this moment forward, our mouth, ears, eyes, hands, feet, yea, our entire body, is no longer ours. We are but the Lord's manager of it. From now on, the two hands, the two feet, the two ears and so forth all belong to the Lord, we having no further right over them.

Interestingly, when a young brother in the Lord died, his elderly father told the pallbearers to be careful in their handling of this corpse because through consecration this body had been the temple of the Holy Spirit for over twenty years. Let us be like that young man and not wait till death comes before presenting our bodies to God. Today the Holy Spirit dwells in us, the Lord already abides in us. And that is why God's word says this in 1 Corinthians 6.19: "Know ye not that your body is a temple of the Holy Spirit which is in you, which ye have from God? and ye are not your own." There is a hymn which has these challenging words:

> *Take my hands, and let them move*
> *At the impulse of Thy love;*
> *Take my feet and let them be*
> *Swift and beautiful for Thee.*
>
> *Take my love; my Lord, I pour*
> *At Thy feet its treasure-store.*
> *Take myself, and I will be*
> *Ever, only, all for Thee.*
>
> —Frances R. Havergal

The words of this hymn are a fitting description of total consecration. It is a presenting of our bodies as living sacrifices. No one can say the body is his. No, in our daily lives our entire bodies are for the Lord; we are but managers over them.

On one Lord's day, when the offering plate came to a thirteen-year-old girl, she asked repeatedly that the plate be lowered. As the plate reached the floor, she stood in it. She had no money, so she gave herself!

Today we too must put our very selves into the offering, as well as persons, works and things. As we put money in on each Lord's day, we put our selves in too. If we leave our selves outside, God will not accept our money. Unless He gets us *ourselves,*

He does not want *ours*. Yet once He has our very *selves*, He will automatically have *ours* as well. Consecration does not necessarily mean to be preachers. The Lord may want you to be good businessmen. We do not choose our particular life's work; we simply tell God that henceforth we will do His will.

The Results of Consecration

What are the results of consecration? One is given in Romans 6, and the other is given in Romans 12. Many do not realize the difference in results, but there is a great difference between these two. In Romans 6, consecration benefits us in that it causes us to bear fruit unto sanctification. In Romans 12, consecration profits God in that His will shall be done. The result of consecration in Romans 6 is that "being made free from sin and become servants to God, ye have your fruit unto sanctification" (v.22). Day by day, you may live a victorious life. The result of consecration in Romans 12, however, is "that ye may prove what is the good and acceptable and perfect will of God" (v.2c).

You should not conclude that with your letting go, believing, and praising, this is enough. There is a final act, which is to put yourself into God's hands that He may manifest His holiness through your body. In the past, you had no strength to consecrate; now having crossed the threshold of victory, you are able to offer up yourself. Please recall that previously you had no way to place yourself in God's hands; now, though, it is no longer a question of ability but a matter of your will. In the earlier days, you *could* not; presently, it is that you *will* not.

A brother in Australia had given himself completely to God. One day on a train some friends needed a partner in playing cards. They asked him to join. His answer to these friends was that he was sorry but he had no hands; for these hands of his no longer belonged to him but to Someone else. Those hands of his were merely appendages to his body; he had no right, nor did he dare, to use them.

You should have the same attitude as this brother, that you dare not use your hands, your feet or your mouth for yourself because they are now the Lord's. Each time you meet a temptation, you should say that you have no hands. This is consecration according to Romans 6. Such consecration sanctifies you and enables you to bear the fruit of holiness. For this reason, consecration should be the first act as well as the first fruit after victory.

Consecration in Romans 12, on the other hand, is for the sake of God: present your body a living sacrifice. Such consecration is holy and is acceptable to Him. Keep in mind here that this consecration is for the purpose of serving God.

Chapter 6 has in view personal sanctification, whereas chapter 12 has in view the matter of the Lord's work. Both chapter 6 and chapter 12 speak of the matter of sanctification or holiness. What is sanctification? It means a being set apart to be used exclusively by a particular person. Formerly, persons and affairs and things could touch me because I was for my own self; now, though, I am wholly for God.

On one occasion I was refused space by a bus driver when I attempted to board his bus at Jessfield Park.* Upon looking carefully, I noticed that it was a charter bus and not a public one. Figuratively speaking, every Christian is chartered, but unfortunately many appear to be like public buses. We are not for public use; we are instead chartered, to be set apart entirely for God's will. Romans 12 shows us that notwithstanding our profession, our husband or wife, our children, money or treasure, all must be wholly and singleheartedly for God. We should present ourselves to Him with singleness of purpose and believe at once that He has accepted us because this is in tune with His will and purpose. God does not seek our fleeting zeal. He will not be satisfied until we offer our very selves entirely to Him. Until we have anointed Him with pure nard, He is not pleased

*A public park in the western section of Shanghai.—*Translator*

(see Mark 14.3). Unless we cast in all the living we have (see Mark 12.44), He is not glorified. Everything must be offered up to God.

We have been raised from the dead and have received the mercies of God. Therefore our consecration is acceptable to Him, and at the same time it is our reasonable service. All Christians, not just special believers, must consecrate themselves. The Lord's blood has bought us; we belong to Him. His love has constrained us, and consequently we want to live for Him.

What kind of sacrifice is it that we offer up to God? According to His word, we are to be living stones, and hence we shall live on; therefore, we are living sacrifices. The sacrifice in the Old Testament period was *killed*, but we today are a *living* sacrifice.

In our thus presenting our bodies, the end result is to be the following: "Be not fashioned according to this world: but be ye transformed by the renewing of your mind, that ye may prove what is the good and acceptable and perfect will of God" (Rom. 12.2). This is the great goal to be arrived at today. In the past we have spoken much about God having an eternal purpose that is to be fulfilled in His Son. His creation, His redemption, His defeat of the devil and His saving of sinners are all for that purpose. Knowing what is the foreordained eternal purpose of God, we may be able to fulfill that which He wants to fulfill. We are here not only for the sake of saving souls. We are here as well for the fulfillment of His purpose.

Without consecration, we cannot possibly see that this will of God is good. Many today are frightened by the very mentioning of God's will. They feel quite uneasy about it and are threatened. Yet Paul testified that once we have presented our bodies as living sacrifices we may prove what is the good and acceptable and perfect will of God. We may sing of the goodness of His will. We may say Hallelujah, His will is truly good. It is good and *not* evil. It is profitable, because God has no evil thought.

How nearsighted we often are. We fail to see the excellency

of God's will. A brother prayed well one day, saying, "Lord, we ask for bread; and we think You will give us a stone. We ask for a fish; and we think You will give us a serpent. We ask for an egg; and we think You will give us a scorpion. But, Lord, when we pray for a stone, what You give is always bread" (see Luke 11.11-12). Often we do not understand God's love and His will. We do not know that His thoughts towards us are peaceful and good—exceedingly good—and not evil (see Jer. 29.10-11). How frequently we murmur for the moment; but probably two years later we will praise Him. Why not praise Him *now?*

God's will is not only good but also perfect. What He has prepared for those who love Him is nothing but what is most profitable. In possession of such knowledge, you will be pleased with His will. You will present your body which is holy and acceptable to God. You will accept His will because you are confident that His will is good and perfect.

May you perform this last act, saying to God from your heart: "O God, I am wholly Yours. Hereafter, I will not live for myself."

By performing this last act, you have now fulfilled all the conditions for victory. Consecration is the first as well as the last facet in this life that wins. Believe that God has accepted your consecration. Once done, it is done. Regardless whether your feeling be cold or hot, as long as you have consecrated with your heart, all is well. I say this to dissuade you one last time from looking at feeling. Henceforth you are the Lord's, and you can only be used by Him.

TITLES YOU
WILL WANT TO HAVE

by Watchman Nee

Basic Lesson Series
Volume 1—A Living Sacrifice
Volume 2—The Good Confession
Volume 3—Assembling Together
Volume 4—Not I, But Christ
Volume 5—Do All to the Glory of God
Volume 6—Love One Another

The Church and the Work
Volume 1—Assembly Life
Volume 2—Rethinking the Work
Volume 3—Church Affairs

The Life That Wins
From Glory to Glory
The Spirit of Judgment
From Faith to Faith
The Lord My Portion
Aids to "Revelation"
Grace for Grace
The Better Covenant
A Balanced Christian Life
The Mystery of Creation
The Messenger of the Cross
Full of Grace and Truth—Volume 1
Full of Grace and Truth—Volume 2
The Spirit of Wisdom and Revelation
Whom Shall I Send?
The Testimony of God
The Salvation of the Soul
The King and the Kingdom of Heaven
The Body of Christ: A Reality
Let Us Pray
God's Plan and the Overcomers
The Glory of His Life
"Come, Lord Jesus"
Practical Issues of This Life
Gospel Dialogue
God's Work
Ye Search the Scriptures
The Prayer Ministry of the Church
Christ the Sum of All Spiritual Things
Spiritual Knowledge
The Latent Power of the Soul
Spiritual Authority
The Ministry of God's Word
Spiritual Reality or Obsession
The Spiritual Man

by Stephen Kaung

Discipled to Christ
The Splendor of His Ways
Seeing the Lord's End in Job
The Songs of Degrees
Meditations on Fifteen Psalms

ORDER FROM:

Christian Fellowship Publishers, Inc.
11515 Allecingie Parkway
Richmond, Virginia 23235